TWENTIETH CENTURY INTERPRETATIONS
OF

CRIME AND PUNISHMENT

A Collection of Critical Essays

Edited by

ROBERT LOUIS JACKSON

Prentice-Hall, Inc.   A SPECTRUM BOOK   *Englewood Cliffs, N.J.*

Library of Congress Cataloging in Publication Data

JACKSON, ROBERT LOUIS, comp.
  Twentieth century interpretations of Crime and punishment.

  (A Spectrum Book)
  Bibliography: 000 p.
    1. Dostoevskii, Fedor Mikhailovich, 1821–1881.
  Prestuplenie i nakazanie—Addresses, essays, lectures.
  I. Title.
  PG3325.P73J3   1974   891.7′3′3   73–15716
  ISBN 0–13–193086–9
  ISBN 0–13–193078–8 (pbk.)

10 9 8 7 6 5 4 3 2 1

PRENTICE-HALL INTERNATIONAL, INC. (*London*)
PRENTICE-HALL OF AUSTRALIA, PTY. LTD. (*Sydney*)
PRENTICE-HALL OF CANADA, LTD. (*Toronto*)
PRENTICE-HALL OF INDIA PRIVATE LIMITED (*New Delhi*)
PRENTICE-HALL OF JAPAN, INC. (*Tokyo*)

Contents

Introduction: The Clumsy White Flower   1
by Robert Louis Jackson

PART ONE—*Into* Crime and Punishment

On *Crime and Punishment* (Letter to Katkov)   9
by Fyodor M. Dostoevsky

Dostoevsky's Search for Motives in the Notebooks
of *Crime and Punishment*   11
by Konstantin Mochulsky

The First Sentence in *Crime and Punishment,* the Word
"Crime," and Other Matters   17
by Vadim V. Kozhinov

Philosophical Pro and Contra in Part One
of *Crime and Punishment*   26
by Robert Louis Jackson

PART TWO—*Two Overviews of* Crime and Punishment

Raskolnikov   41
by Jacques Madaule

A Great Philosophical Novel   49
by Nicholas M. Chirkov

PART THREE—*The Metaphysical Point of View*

The Problem of Evil   71
by Nicholas Berdyaev

The Problem of Guilt   77
by Alfred L. Bem

PART FOUR—*The World of* Crime and Punishment

The World of Raskolnikov   81
   by Joseph Frank

Raskolnikov's Theory on the "Rights" of Great Men and
   Napoleon III's *History of Caesar*   91
   by F. I. Evnin

PART FIVE—*Ends and Beginnings*

Toward Regeneration   94
   by Yury F. Karyakin

The Death of Svidrigailov   103
   by Aron Z. Steinberg

The Death of Marmeladov   106
   by Konrad Onasch

Disease as Dialectic in *Crime and Punishment*   109
   by James M. Holquist

Chronology of Important Dates   *119*
Notes on the Editor and Contributors   *120*
Selected Bibliography   *122*

Then I realized, Sonia, that if one waits for every one to get wiser it will take too long. What's more, I realized that that would never come to pass, that people won't change, and nobody can reform them, and it's not worth the effort! Yes, that's so! That's the law of their nature*** Their law, Sonia! That's so! (V, 4)

And now I have only come to say (Dunia began to get up) that if you should happen to need me, or need***all my life, or anything*** you must call me, and I will come. Good-bye! (V, 5)

Introduction:
The Clumsy White Flower

by Robert Louis Jackson

In the early part of *Crime and Punishment* (*Prestuplenie i nakazanie,* 1866), just after the murder, Raskolnikov is lying in bed. People around him are discussing the crime. Nastasia, the servant girl, at one point remarks that the pawnbroker's sister Lizaveta (the second but unintended victim of Raskolnikov) was murdered, too.

> "Lizaveta?" Raskolnikov murmured in a scarcely audible voice. "You know. Lizaveta. She used to sell things. Once in a while she used to come here. Even mended a shirt for you once." Raskolnikov turned to the wall. He turned to the dirty yellow strips of wallpaper decorated with white flowers, and he chose one clumsy white flower with brownish veins and started examining it: how many leaves it had, and the cut of the scalloped edges of the leaves, and how many veins in each leaf. He felt his arms and legs go numb, as if they had been removed. He did not even try to move, but stared obstinately at the flower. (II, 4) [1]

R. P. Blackmur rightly singled out this passage for its dramatic content.[2] The "clumsy white flower" in its dirty yellow setting (yellow is the color of crime in this novel [3]) is a fitting symbol of the awkward and innocent Lizaveta. Raskolnikov's shock of recognition, as he absentmindedly focuses on this image, brings home to the reader what the murderer momentarily experiences in his whole being: the human reality of murder, the realization that killing is not arithmetic, the awareness that all life is

---

[1] In all of the essays in this volume (excepting those by Mochulsky, Frank and Holquist) major quotations and most minor ones from Dostoevsky's novel refer to Sidney Monas' translation of *Crime and Punishment* (New York: Signet Classics, 1968). Here and there, for reasons usually connected with the context, I have made some small changes. Roman and Arabic numerals following quotations refer respectively to the major division (Part) and chapter in which the quotation appears.

[2] R. P. Blackmur, "*Crime and Punishment:* Murder in Your Own Room," in *Eleven Essays in the European Novel* (New York, Harcourt, Brace & World, Inc., 1964), p. 129.

[3] See Vadim V. Kozhinov's discussion of the color yellow in *Crime and Punishment* on pages 19–20 of this collection.

sacred. But the moment is a passing one for Raskolnikov. More often Raskolnikov defends his crime to himself and others, attempts to place himself above and beyond its deeper moral meaning. Some force that we call "conscience" or "guilt" (but that requires much more precise definition) does seem to drive him inexorably to confess his crime; some inner force does track him down, compels him to seek out his persecutors and, finally, turn himself in. The verisimilitude of this whole inner process—the fact that we recognize it as true to Raskolnikov's character but also to human nature—is one of Dostoevsky's great triumphs in the novel. But, as the reader also knows, Raskolnikov never admits that he was *wrong* until the epilogue, and then only in a symbolic gesture, at the end of about nine months in prison, when he falls at the feet of Sonia in an access of love and almost cosmic awareness.[4] Until that moment, however, his state of intellectual consciousness closely resembles that of the man from the "underground" (*Notes from the Underground*, 1864) who feels "guilty but without guilt before the laws of nature." Raskolnikov feels no remorse, although Dostoevsky speaks of his awareness of a "profound lie" within himself. He can find no terrible guilt in his past, except for "what was simply a *blunder*, the sort of thing that might happen to anyone." He is ashamed only that he has "come to grief so blindly, hopelessly, deafly and stupidly, by some decree of blind fate, and had to resign himself to such 'meaninglessness' and make the best of such a decree if he wanted any peace at all for himself." Raskolnikov acknowledges that he violated the criminal code—but that is all. "Why does what I committed seem so hideous to them?" he said to himself. "Because it was a crime? What does that word mean—'crime'? [5] My conscience is at rest."

Crime: what does that word mean? That is what *Crime and Punishment* is about. The particular horror of Raskolnikov's crime—as well as its interest from a psychological point of view—is in that bland question and in the stubborn answer: my conscience is easy. Is there such a thing as evil or evil-doing? Is there an inner law of conscience—corresponding, or giving expression to, a moral or divine Law—which one can violate only at the risk of psychic self-destruction and (in macrocosmic terms) of apocalypse? That is, perhaps, the fundamental question posed in *Crime and Punishment*. Dostoevsky's answer, through his characterizations of

---

[4] The approximately "nine months" of maturation in prison-exile end precisely in a *birth* of a new Raskolnikov (an idea expressed even in the fact that "suddenly something seemed to seize him and hurl him to her feet"). The birth of a potentially new Raskolnikov is the central event of Chapter Two in the epilogue, just as, symbolically, the central event in Chapter One of the epilogue is the illness and death of his mother.

[5] The word Raskolnikov uses for "crime" here—in place of the usual *"prestuplenie,"* which means both transgression and a criminal act in the legal sense—is *"zlodejanie,"* literally, "evil-doing." Raskolnikov knows, of course, the moral as well as legal meaning of the word *"prestuplenie"* (literally, a "stepping over"); his choice of the more metaphysical word here is partly evasive; but it also serves to underscore the difficult problem he (as well as Dostoevsky) is grappling with in the novel: what is evil?

Raskolnikov and (though more ambiguously) Svidrigailov, is that such a law exists and that we violate it at the expense of our humanity and all humanity.

Crime and Punishment is not just about tabloid-type murders (though it is about these, too) and legal punishment. It is about people who morally "step over," or transgress; people who arrogate to themselves the "right" to transgress. In one of his notebooks, Dostoevsky speaks of the theme of the novel as involving a "theoretical" crime. As the Soviet Russian critic Yury F. Karyakin rightly observes in this connection, the "main murderer" for Dostoevsky is the one who provides the ideological groundwork or justification for murder: "Ideologists for him bear the heaviest burden of responsibility, in any case no less responsibility than that borne by the politicians. Dostoevsky understood that for certain externally attractive and seemingly convincing syllogisms mankind must pay in blood." [6] To this truth, of course, the twentieth century bears grim witness.

The ethical question of the novel is whether man has the right to commit vile acts for good ends, whether any end, however beneficial to man, can justify inhuman means. Dostoevsky is adamant in his answer: the end can never justify the means. But as the Soviet scholar, Nicholas Vilmont, observes, *Crime and Punishment* is also about the obverse of this same question: "is it possible, in general, to subordinate all of one's behavior and acts to the moral law, to unconditional duty, to 'God's truth,' while living miserably in a thoroughly immoral society, one which is corrupt and which corrupts man? Dostoevsky is absolutely firm in his answer: *granted that it is impossible, yet one must, unconditionally!* Because—as Natorp correctly notes, 'the concepts of duty, honor and conscience are unshakeable for him'." [7] *Crime and Punishment* explores— one might say, suffers—the full range of this paradox: the crime of Raskolnikov, arising as it does from a deep, though muddled humanism, suggests both the extreme difficulty of adhering to this moral injunction and yet the need unconditionally to affirm it. The whole novel constitutes an affirmation of moral law. The "answer," of course, to the terrible paradoxes, the moral problems, and contradictions raised by Raskolnikov, or dramatized in the lives of Marmeladov, Sonia, Katerina Ivanovna, Dunia, and others, does not for Dostoevsky lie in the realm of moral logic or dialectic. It lies in the acceptance and organic realization in one's own life, and in the life of mankind of a higher truth: the necessity of love and the willingness to make oneself vulnerable in its expression. It is noteworthy that after his emotional reconciliation with Sonia in the epilogue, Raskolnikov cannot concentrate his thought or think for long on

---

[6] Jurij F. Karjakin, "O filosofsko-eticheskoj problematike romana *Prestuplenie i nakazanie*" ["Philosophical and Ethical Problems in *Crime and Punishment*"] in *Dostoevskij i ego vremja* [*Dostoevsky and His Time*] (Leningrad, 1971), p. 167.

[7] Nikolaj N. Vil'mont, "Dostoevskij i Shiller" ["Dostoevsky and Schiller"] in *Velikie sputniki* [*Great Companions*] (Moscow, 1966), p. 192.

anything; ["nor could he indeed consciously resolve anything; he was simply feeling. Life had replaced dialectic; and something quite different now had to be worked out in his consciousness." These lines are among the most important in the novel.]

What gives *Crime and Punishment* its permanent interest for the reader, of course, is the fearless manner in which Dostoevsky poses fundamental moral, social, and philosophical questions, and leaves them open, even as he points to their resolution. The Soviet Russian critic Vadim V. Kozhinov goes so far as to say that *Crime and Punishment* is a novel of "insoluble questions." [8] Less categorical in judgment, but no less aware of the protean character of *Crime and Punishment,* the great Russian poet Alexander Blok long ago suggested that Dostoevsky did not utter "an unequivocal 'no' " to Raskolnikov's nihilism; moreover, he felt that Dostoevsky was "enamored" of his creation Svidrigailov. The enigmatic Svidrigailov is, in any case, the entrance into the novel's deepest moral and philosophical labyrinths. Dostoevsky's deep, almost desperate concern with Svidrigailov as a type, and his final judgment of him, is plain: he represents, in his indifference to good and evil, his moral cynicism, his conscious embodiment of the principle that "all is permissible" ("Tell me, why should I restrain myself?"), the last degree of sickness in the moral universe.

Yet the obverse of Svidrigailov's indifference to good and evil may be taken as man's openness to every possible experience in the universe. "I am a man, *et nihil humanum,*" [9] Svidrigailov observes at one point in defense of his excesses. To be a man, a human being—as Svidrigailov interprets the well-known observation of Terence—is to be beyond good and evil; that is, to recognize our "humanness" (for Svidrigailov our likeness to "nature") is to obviate any specifically "moral" judgment. This was not, of course, Dostoevsky's point of view. To be human, for Dostoevsky, was precisely to evaluate experience and action in moral terms. The Russian critic Vissarion Belinsky, Dostoevsky wrote, "knew that the moral principle is at the root of everything." Yet the Soviet Russian scholar N. M. Chirkov is undoubtedly correct in finding in Svidrigailov a variant of what he calls Dostoevsky's *"chelovek-univers"*—man as a "universe in miniature," an example of a type that gives evidence of man's extraordinary "capacity for the most diverse and contradictory actions, a capacity for everything, both good and evil." [10] "A thousand times I have been amazed at this capacity of man (and, it seems, chiefly Russian man)," remarks the narrator-hero of *The Raw Youth,* "for cher-

---

[8] See Kozhinov's discussion of the matter on pages 17–19 of his essay in this collection.

[9] The whole saying is: *"Homo sum, et nihil humanum a me alienum puto"*—"I am a man and nothing human is alien to me."

[10] For a discussion of Chirkov's concept of the so-called *"chelovek-univers"* ["man-universe"] in Dostoevsky's work, see my footnote to Chirkov's essay in this collection on page 61.

ishing in his soul the most lofty ideal side by side with the most extreme vileness, and all this absolutely sincerely. Whether this is a special breadth in Russian man which will lead him far, or simply vileness—that is the question!" (Part III, chap. 3, sec. 1) This question also lies at the basis of the characterization of Svidrigailov.

Svidrigailov is baffling. What is disturbing about him is not only that he can commit such terrible crimes, but that the same man can appear so much "like us all," so charming, so knowledgeable, so restrained in judgment; so "good" in letting Dunia go (VI, 5), and so generous in his final role as "benefactor" of the Marmeladov family (in fact, in this role he succeeds precisely where Raskolnikov fails); indeed, in the words of Goethe's Mephistopheles he emerges almost melodramatically as "part of that force that always wills evil and always creates good" ("Ein Teil von jener Kraft, Die stets das Böse will und stets das Gute schafft"). And all this "absolutely sincerely"!

In short, Svidrigailov strikes us as "human" in the full range of his nature—a nature, however, that has cut loose from all Christian precepts and morality. The ambivalence of Dostoevsky's approach to Svidrigailov, then, consists in the fact that while his final judgment and resolution of the character Svidrigailov is profoundly moral, his basic characterization of him tends to lift him, as a type, into some new category of men who thrive "beyond good and evil" and who seem to elude rectilinear evaluation as "bad." A psychological interpretation of good and evil seems, at this level of characterization, to have been substituted for an ethical interpretation. Such is the paradoxical and perhaps revolutionary character of Dostoevsky's creation Svidrigailov. He went very far in the exploration of a type that clearly approaches, conceptually, Nietzsche's *Übermensch* (overman). But whereas Nietzsche perfects and idealizes this type, Dostoevsky deliberately draws him back into the circle of Hebraic-Christian morality and judgment, revealing his all-too-human nature.

There can be no authentic existence, Dostoevsky insists, beyond good and evil. He constantly reaffirms his belief in the necessity of an aesthetic and spiritual ideal in the life of man and of the need for a tension toward that ideal. "Human nature unfailingly demands something to worship," Dostoevsky observed in one of his notebooks. And his Grand Inquisitor (*The Brothers Karamazov*) unquestionably expresses Dostoevsky's view when he observes that "the secret of human existence is not only in living, but in knowing why one lives. Without a clear idea of what to live for man will not consent to live and will rather destroy himself than remain on earth." The absolutely autonomous existence, the life of the man-god, raised above the life and needs of ordinary men, was, Dostoevsky believed, not only inhuman but antihuman and ultimately self-destructive. There is a rigorous logic to the suicide of Svidrigailov as his vain hope of salvation through Dunia vanishes.

"What is evil," asks the French Catholic historian Jacques Madaule, "if not suffering inflicted gratuitously, and as though out of pleasure on an innocent creature? Such is absolute evil." [11] And it is precisely in his indifference to good and evil, in his gratuitous inflicting of suffering upon the innocent, that we recognize in Svidrigailov the poisoned herald of our century; and not merely of the modern individualist who has become a law unto himself, but of whole societies that in full self-consciousness, and Christian consciousness, and in a state of maximum security and freedom (and sometimes also of boredom) have *chosen* to transgress, arrogantly and mercilessly, like Napoleon, to "punish the peoples," to inflict suffering and disaster upon the innocent. Here Raskolnikov's crime is also relevant: a "theoretical" crime, murder for an "idea," murder, paradoxically, out of love for humanity; and along with this paradox, there is that sneaking realm of consciousness between the vague feeling of guilt and the inability to feel remorse, that stubborn habit (which Raskolnikov shares with so many of Dostoevsky's heroes) of blaming circumstances and "fate" instead of recognizing the ancient Greek truth that a man's character is his fate.

Raskolnikov's crime, in the final analysis, is paradigmatic of the human condition: what man is. Yet *Crime and Punishment,* as we have noted, is also a novel about suffering, guilt and the possibility of a new consciousness, a novel about *man becoming.* Raskolnikov's final experience of the truth in the epilogue is an epiphany made possible by the presence in Raskolnikov in the deepest sources of his childhood experience, and in the people about him, of forces for good. What Raskolnikov finally experiences the reader has already "learned" through his reading of the novel.

The epilogue is not a didactic supplement or artificial "appendix" to *Crime and Punishment*: it is the summing up of the central issues and processes of novel and character in ideological, spiritual and mythic terms —as Yury F. Karyakin and James M. Holquist bring out in their discussion of the epilogue.[12] The epilogue, finally, is the transformation of ends into beginnings. Konstantin Mochulsky rightly represents the murder of the old pawnbroker and Lizaveta in Part One of the novel, in dramatic terms, as a prologue followed by a tragedy in five acts, and an epilogue. But on the metaphysical plane of the novel, this prologue, with its act of murder, is really an epilogue, or fall, whereas the formal epilogue serves as the prologue for a new drama and new life. Thus, at the conclusion of the novel the reader finds Raskolnikov, like Milton's Adam, on his lofty hill, on the "high bank" overlooking the steppe:

> A scarcely audible song wafted from the far bank. There on the boundless steppe, flooded with sunshine, the black dots of nomad tents could be barely seen. There freedom was; and people lived who were quite different

[11] See Jacques Madaule's essay in this collection on page 41.
[12] See the essays of Karyakin and Holquist in this collection.

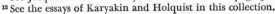

from the people on his side of the river. There time seemed to have stood still, as though the age of Abraham and his flock had not passed. (Epilogue, 2)

The moment of vision, in which past and future merge in the present, immediately precedes Raskolnikov's moment of reconciliation with Sonia. This overcoming of temporal time in the timeless vision, this passing beyond crime and punishment into a new realm of consciousness where "something quite different" had to be worked out, this transformation of epilogue into prologue is one of the greatest moments of the novel— a moment in which the meaning of the novel and the meaning of art at their deepest levels, are identical; an epiphany the truth of which Dostoevsky found in man's historical consciousness and eternal quest for the ideal.

"Raskolnikoff [13] is easily the greatest book I have read in ten years," Robert Louis Stevenson wrote in a letter to J. A. Symonds in the spring of 1886. "I am glad you took to it. Many find it dull: Henry James could not finish it: all I can say is, it nearly finished me. It was like having an illness." Among Dostoevsky's works, *Crime and Punishment* has in the past evoked the most extensive and—like Stevenson's—the most passionate responses from readers and critics. Russian, European, and American sources combine in this collection to bring before the reader original criticism and essays, mostly untranslated until now. A concentration on the philosophical, moral, psychological, and social problems raised by *Crime and Punishment* distinguishes this collection.

With Dostoevsky's own statement of intention as a nucleus, the first group of essays broadens out to include his struggle to clarify the "motives" of the crime in his notebooks (Mochulsky); a consideration of the first sentence in the novel and the concept of the word "crime" in Russian (Kozhinov); a close analysis of Part One and of the moral-philosophical issues underlying Raskolnikov's crime (Jackson). The second group of essays (Madaule and Chirkov) provides the reader with intensive critical analysis of the major problems and characters in the novel, whereas the third group (Berdyaev and Bem) examines the crucial questions of evil and guilt from a metaphysical point of view. The final section shows how the epilogue and the deaths of Marmeladov and Svidrigailov embody Dostoevsky's thought.

The essayists in this collection represent a broad critical spectrum. We may distinguish three periods of criticism after the death of Dostoevsky: philosophical criticism extending into the 1920s (Rozanov, Ivanov, Shestov, and Berdyaev); the early Soviet period of the 1920s, when such Soviet scholars as Grossman, Dolinin, and Bakhtin focused on important literary, historical, and stylistic studies; and the post-Stalin period, involving a re-

---

[13] Stevenson first read *Crime and Punishment* in a French translation.

assessment of the ideological quarantine of Dostoevsky that existed during the Stalin era.

Nicholas Berdyaev, the outstanding Russian philosopher who emigrated to the West after the Bolshevik Revolution, is a signal representative of the school of philosophical criticism, with its metaphysical and ontological orientation. His study, *Dostoevsky* (1923), is itself part of Russian cultural history. Berdyaev's discussion on "evil"—presented here in a new translation—remains one of the best introductions to the metaphysics of *Crime and Punishment*. The philosophical school and the craftsmanlike Soviet scholarship of the 1920s both contributed to the fine writings of Alfred L. Bem and Konstantin Mochulsky, Russian emigré scholars. Aron Z. Steinberg belongs to this group of writers.

The arid period of Stalinism in the Soviet Union (1930s and 1940s) was particularly uncongenial for Dostoevsky scholarship and criticism. Dostoevsky's work was not published extensively; it was frequently denigrated or ignored in textbooks and officially inspired pronouncements. Nicholas M. Chirkov may justly be singled out as one of the more talented and faithful of the "monks" of Dostoevsky scholarship in this period. His studies on Dostoevsky, written then, began to appear only in the 1960s. His thoughtful essay on *Crime and Punishment,* so responsive to the ideological complexity of Dostoevsky, is a compact introduction to the novel, as well as a noteworthy example of sociological criticism that transcends narrow dogmatism.

During the period since Stalin's death in 1953, valuable scholarly work has been accomplished, although, occasionally, zealous efforts to "recapture" Dostoevsky for socialist humanism have involved a new simplification of the dense and difficult texture of his work. Among the gifted critics and scholars of the recent period, Vadim V. Kozhinov, in his extended essay on *Crime and Punishment* seems to synthesize some of the achievements of the Russian formalist traditions of the 1920s with an understanding of social and philosophical elements. F. I. Evnin and Yury F. Karyakin are among a number of Soviet Dostoevsky scholars (including Fridlender, Bursov, Kirpotin, Belov, Grigoriev and Rosenblum) who are continuing the sober traditions of early Soviet scholarship.

A diversity of points of view is reflected in the Western scholars in this collection: Jacques Madaule, with his literary perceptiveness and moral clarity; Konrad Onasch, with his interest in the religious ethos in Dostoevsky; and James M. Holquist, with his receptiveness to contemporary literary and anthropological thought. Joseph Frank approaches Dostoevsky through an informed analysis of the ideological and cultural context of the novel. The editor of this volume focuses upon its philosophical and psychological aspects.

On *Crime and Punishment*
(Letter to M. N. Katkov)

by Fyodor M. Dostoevsky

This is the psychological account of a crime. The action is contemporary, taking place in the present year. A young man, expelled from the student body of the university, of lower-class origins and living in utter poverty through thoughtlessness, through an infirmity of notions, having come under the influence of some of those strange, "incomplete" ideas which go floating about in the air, has decided to break out of his loathsome situation in one stroke. He has decided to kill a certain old woman, the widow of a titular councilor, who lends out money at interest. The old woman is stupid, hard of hearing, sickly, and greedy. She demands a Jew's percentage, is malicious, and tears other people's lives to pieces, harassing her own younger sister like a factory worker. "She is not fit for anything," "What does she live for?" "Is she of use to anyone at all?" etc. These questions thoroughly disconcert the young man. He decides to kill her, to rob her of everything in order to bring happiness to his mother, who is living in the provinces; to save his sister, who lives with some landowners as a paid companion, from the lascivious claims of the head of this landowning family—claims which are threatening her with ruin; to finish his studies; to go abroad; and then for the remainder of his entire life to be honorable, upright, steadfast in fulfilling "his humane debt to mankind," which will, of course, "expiate his crime," if in fact the term crime can be applied to this act directed against an old woman, deaf, stupid, evil, and ailing, who herself does not know why she continues living on this earth and who after a month, perhaps, would die anyway of her own accord. Despite the fact that crimes of this nature are terribly difficult to perpetrate—i.e., some traces, clues, and so forth are almost always quite grossly evident and an enormous amount is left to chance, which almost always betrays the guilty party—it happens that in an absolutely fortuitous fashion he succeeds in accomplishing his undertaking

"On Crime and Punishment *(Letter to M. N. Katkov)"* [*Editor's title*] *by Fyodor M. Dostoevsky. Excerpt from a draft of a letter by Dostoevsky to M. N. Katkov. From Konstantin Mochulsky,* Dostoevsky: His Life and Work, *translated by Michael A. Minihan (copyright © 1967 by Princeton University Press; Princeton Paperback, 1971), pp. 272–273. Reprinted by permission of Princeton University Press.*

both quickly and successfully. He passes almost a month after that before the final catastrophe. No one is suspicious of him, nor can they be. And so it is here that the whole psychological process of the crime unfolds. Insoluble questions confront the murderer; unsuspected and unanticipated feelings torment his heart. Divine truth and justice, the earthly law, claim their rights, and he ends by being *compelled* to give himself up. Compelled so that even if he perish in penal servitude, nonetheless he might once again be united to men. The feeling that he is separated and cut off from mankind, which he experienced immediately upon the completion of the crime, has tortured him. The law of justice and human nature have taken their hold. . . . The criminal himself decides to accept suffering in order to atone for his deed. But then I find it difficult to elucidate my thought fully. In my story there is, moreover, a hint of the idea that the criminal is much less daunted by the established legal punishment for a crime than lawgivers think, partly because *he himself experiences a moral need for it*. I have observed this even in the most undeveloped people, in the most crude circumstances. I wanted to express this idea particularly in a developed individual of the new generation so that the thought might be more clearly and concretely seen. Several incidents which have occurred quite recently have convinced me that *my subject* is not at all eccentric. Especially that the murderer is an intellectually developed young man who even has good inclinations. Last year in Moscow I was told (this is actually true) about a certain student expelled from the University after the incident with the Moscow students, that he decided to break into a post office and kill the postman. In our papers there are still many traces of this unusual infirmity of notions which is materializing into terrible deeds. (That seminarian who killed a girl in a barn after an agreement with her, and whom they arrested an hour later at lunch, and so forth.) In a word, I feel convinced that my subject is justified in part by contemporary life. . . ."

Dostoevsky's Search for Motives
in the Notebooks for *Crime and Punishment*

by Konstantin Mochulsky

We are in possession of three notebooks with rough drafts and notations for *Crime and Punishment*.[1] They are spread over a period between September 1865 and February 1866. It is difficult to reestablish the precise chronological sequence of the notes since the author made notations in different books simultaneously, interspersing them with calculations as to how much he should realize from the edition, with entries of his pressing debts and of addresses, with sketches of persons and buildings and words written out in calligraphic form: Napoléon, Julius Caesar, Rachel. . . .

For a long time the fundamental idea of the novel continued to puzzle its author. In his sketchbooks he is constantly returning to the question: why did Raskolnikov commit the murder? And his answers are varied. We feel it possible to relate this complicated motivation to two basic ideas. The first of these corresponds to the original plan for the *tale* and is expounded in the letter to Katkov. It borders upon the concept of Rastignac in Balzac's novel *Père Goriot*: may not a man do something which in itself is a small evil, for the sake of accomplishing a great good; may he not kill one insignificant and pernicious being in order to bring happiness to many worthy people who otherwise are going to perish? Does a noble end justify illicit means? Can a man through his own will set aright the ways of Providence? In accord with this idea Raskolnikov imagines himself to be a magnanimous idealist, a humanist thirsting to bring happiness to all mankind. His heart which is noble and compassionate, is pierced by the spectacle of human suffering. In the past, at the cost of great personal sacrifice, he had tried many times to help the "humiliated and wronged."

"*Dostoevsky's Search for Motives in the Notebooks for* Crime and Punishment" [*Editor's title*], *by Konstantin Mochulsky. From Konstantin Mochulsky*, Dostoevsky: His Life and Work, *translated by Michael A. Minihan (Princeton: copyright © 1967 by Princeton University Press, Princeton Paperback, 1971), pp. 278; 280–286. Reprinted by permission of the Princeton University Press.*

[1] Central Archives, *Iz Arkhiva F. M. Doestoevskogo. Prestuplenie i nakazanie. Neizdannye materialy.* (From the Archives of F. M. Dostoevsky, *Crime and Punishment. Unpublished Materials.*) Prepared for printing by I. N. Glivenko. Moscow-Leningrad, 1931.

But the idealist arrives at the realization that he is utterly powerless when confronted with world evil. Humility and sacrifice are fruitless; good is completely ineffectual. Good people are continually perishing, while evil ones flourish. And then, in despair, he decides to "transgress" the moral law. This dialectic leads him to his crime: he kills a human being for love of humanity; he perpetrates evil for love of good. In the notebooks we find the "idea of Rastignac" developed at great length. Raskolnikov says: "By my very nature I cannot simply stand by and allow a miscreant to bring some poor, defenseless being to ruin. I will interfere. I want to interfere. And that is why I want power. . . ." "I am seizing power, I'm securing force—whether it be money or sheer might—not for evil. I bear happiness. Oh, why isn't everyone happy? A picture of the golden age. It's already borne in minds and hearts. How can one not want to have it come about!" The author has imparted to the murderer his own dream about the "golden age"! And in another place: "His prayer upon coming back from the Marmeladovs. (briefly) Lord! If this attempt upon an old woman who is blind, stupid, not really needed by anyone, is a sin, considering the fact that I wanted to devote myself, then blame and convict me. I have judged myself exactingly; this is not vain pride. . . . And then after I have become noble, the benefactor of all, a citizen, I will repent (*he prayed to Christ,* lay down)."

Raskolnikov seeks power not because of his vanity; he consecrates himself to the service of mankind. He realizes that his act is a sin, and knowingly he takes it upon himself. He prays to Christ, and believes in repentance and expiation. "Poor mother, my poor sister," he says, "I wanted this for you. If there is a sin here, I resolved to take it upon myself, but only so that you might be happy." The author is fascinated by the acute paradox that lies in murder for the sake of others, in the desire for might and money in the name of complete altruism. Raskolnikov is not the executioner but the victim. He has shed another's blood, but he would have been capable of shedding his own as well. "To Sonya: 'Love! And is it possible that I do not love, if I have decided to take such a horrible thing upon myself? So what that it's someone else's blood and not my own? *And would I not give all my blood if it were necessary?*' He stopped and reflected. 'Before God Who sees me and before my conscience, talking with myself here, I say: I would give it.' "

This extraordinary entry gives us the definitive formula for the *idea of murder motivated by love.* Faced with such a conception of the hero, *Crime and Punishment* ought to have been transformed into *Crime and Expiation.* Raskolnikov, who believes in God, who prays to Christ, but who has gone astray because of his love, must be saved. The author presents an outline that suggests a fortuitous denouement. "This very crime itself gives rise to his moral evolution, to the possibility of such questions as formerly would never have entered his mind. In the last chapter while he is serving his sentence of penal servitude, he remarks that without this crime he would never have realized such questions, desires, feelings, needs, aspirations, and development." In this way the crime becomes the source of his moral rebirth and leads to the criminal's spiritual restoration. Expiation can begin even before he is sent to the penal colony.

In one rough draft the following plan is indicated: after his confession to Sonya, Raskolnikov wanders about the streets. "A whirlwind. *A vision of Christ.*" Christ Himself comes to save the sinner who has repented. After this mystical encounter the hero chances upon a fire. "At the fire he accomplished resounding deeds (he saved someone from death). He arrives home all scorched. His mother, his sister are at his bedside. He makes his peace with everyone. His joy, the joyous evening. 'Now the only thing that matters is that you will expiate everything by heroism, you will redeem everything' (the words of Sonya)." Traces of this plan have come down to us even in the final printed text: the vision of Christ has been replaced by the reading of the Gospel with Sonya; the episode with the fire and "heroism" is transferred back to the past. At the trial Raskolnikov's landlady testified that "when earlier they were living in another house, at Five Corners, there was a fire at night and her lodger pulled two small children out of one of the apartments which had already caught fire, and was then badly burned." Finally the repentant criminal kisses the ground and goes to give himself up. "Sonya and love have conquered!"

But the author was not content with the "idea of Rastignac" and the image of the altruistic murderer. He penetrates the criminal's soul and discovers there even greater depths. Behind the idea that a noble heart has gone astray there lies hidden another idea, majestic and terrible. For the purposes of a schema one could call it *"the idea of Napoleon."* Raskolnikov divides mankind into two unequal parts: the majority—this is a "trembling creature" whose role is to obey; and the minority, composed of those people "who have power," who stand above the law (Napoleon). His committing the murder had no bearing at all upon love for mankind; he killed to find out "whether he was a louse or a man." The idea of Rastignac and that of Napoleon, in spite of their exterior resemblance (the transgression of the moral law), inwardly are diametrically opposed. According to the first, Raskolnikov's deed is an error executed in the name of the most noble intentions; according to the second, it is an objective crime, a revolt against the divine order of the world, the self-exaltation of the strong personality. In the first design, the murderer is a humanist and a Christian who acknowledges his sin and redeems it by repentance and suffering; in the second, he is an atheist, a *demonic personality,* not bound by conscience, who is incapable of repentance and rebirth.

The "idea of Napoleon" took hold of Dostoevsky. Parallel to the motif of love for mankind, he developed the motif of hate and contempt for them. Raskolnikov says: "How vile men are! Are they worth bowing down before and asking forgiveness? No, no, I will keep silent. . . . But with what *contempt*. How base, how vile men are. No: to gather them into one's arm, and then to do good for them. . . . Is it possible to love them? Is it possible to suffer for them? *Hatred for mankind*." The strong individual wishes power and only power. It is irrelevant what use he makes of this power; it does not matter whether he will turn it to man's good or to evil. There is only one thing that is important: *power for power's sake*. Humane motives are a lie and a deceit; truth is the metaphysical will to might. The murderer declares to Sonya: " 'Whatever I may be, whatever then I may do, whether I benefit mankind or I suck the living juices from it like a spider—this is my own affair. I know that I want to *dominate,* and that is enough. . . .' 'In what does happiness lie then?' said Sonya. 'Happiness is *power,*' he said." Another variant of this conversation with Sonya: "He says: 'To rule over them.' All this meanness and baseness on every side only angers him. *An utter contempt for people. Pride.* He informs Sonya of his contempt for people. He does not wish to stoop to argue with her." The pride of the man-godhead is underlined in the following note: "To Sonya: 'But I had to take the first step. I must have power. I cannot . . . *I want everything that I see to be different than it is.* Up till now that was all I needed. I even committed murder. After that *more is needed.* . . . I myself want to act. I don't know how far I will go. I don't want to submit myself to anyone.' " A man sets himself in place of God and wants to reorder all of creation. Murder is only the beginning of the revolt; "after that more is needed." It is impossible to say to what measure of evil he will go. His demonic path is only indicated by the author: "How base men are. *Dream about a new crime.*" Dostoevsky halted before this abyss; Raskolnikov will not commit new crimes. But how will it all end? The fortuitous denouement which was suited to the "idea of Rastignac," is of course out of the question. The demonic personality cannot come to repentance and rebirth; it is doomed to perdition. Dostoevsky noted: *"Finale of the novel. Raskolnikov goes to shoot himself."* The hero's suicide was to have taken place immediately after Marmeladov's death. "Marmeladov's death. A bullet in the forehead."

The writer found himself faced with an insoluble dilemma: two opposing ideas were contending for his hero's fate. He could see two possible solutions to his problem: either to sacrifice one for the sake of the other or find some synthesis which would encompass both. It seems that for some time he was inclined to follow the first alternative. One entry reads: "The main anatomy of the novel: after the sickness and so on, it is of the utmost importance to direct the course of affairs onto a real climax and do away with this vagueness, i.e., *explain the murder in one manner or another* and establish his character and attitudes clearly. . . . Conflict with reality and the logical outcome of the law of nature and of duty." In other words, the author intended to discard the "idea of Napoleon" and bring his hero to a spiritual rebirth. . . . But this would have entailed impoverishing and simplifying the design. Dostoevsky chose the more difficult way out: to employ both ideas, to join them in a single soul, to portray the hero's conscience in its tragic duality. This almost impossible task was ingeniously realized in the novel. Originally, the murderer's true character was to be disclosed after Marmeladov's death at Razumikhin's soirée. At the requiem service[2] for the civil servant who was run down by horses, Raskolnikov experiences an influx of remorse and contrition, but it is followed by new affirmations of self: "He goes to Razumikhin's. The soirée. He arrives, having experienced contrition, and there follows *demonic pride*. Completely on the defense." In another variation, Marmeladov's death only serves to intensify his awareness of his own righteousness: "He went to Marmeladov's requiem service. . . . Shaken, confirmed, and proud, he goes to the soirée at Razumikhin's. *Devil-like pride*." Exposing the hero as a demon ought to be an effective *coup de maître*. "So here there is a *coup de maître*. At first there was apprehension, then fear and terror, and his character was not completely unmasked, and here suddenly his whole character unveiled itself in all its *demonic force* and all the reasons and motives for the crime become understandable. . . . The full import of this must come out at Razumikhin's soirée in his *satanic pride*." "The soirée at Razumikhin's *(terrible pride)*. . . . In the novel the concept of *exorbitant pride*, of arrogance and contempt for this society is expressed in his image. His idea: to seize power over this society. Despotism is his characteristic trait. To express all this at Razumikhin's soirée." Pride (demonic, devil-like, satanic) is insistently underlined. Love for mankind proves to be only a mask; contempt and despotism lie hidden beneath it. In view of such a conception, the proposed finale with the fire and the hero's surrendering himself to the police takes on quite another sense. Raskolnikov is punishing himself because of his weakness and cowardliness, but he does not repent. He turns himself over to the authorities out of *contempt*. "Pride, his arrogance and conviction of his own guiltlessness continually go *crescendo* and suddenly at its strongest phase, after the fire, he goes to give himself up." The most terrible thing of all is that this demonic force does not disroot his humanism. Under the psychological stratum an even deeper layer is uncovered—a metaphysical one. And before this profundity the psychological level is exposed as a false mask. *Raskolnikov is a demon embodied in a humanist.*

The "demon's" path leads to perdition; the way of the humanist who has sinned and then repented, brings salvation. But what of the path of the demon who is embodied in a humanist, of the man in whom "two

---

[2] A *Panikhida* is a service of prayer for the repose of the departed's soul (not a Divine Liturgy or "mass") held on the third, ninth, and fortieth days after death. It is also customary to celebrate *panikhidi* on the anniversaries of the departed's birth-day, name-day and death-day.

opposing characters" are merged (Razumikhin's words regarding Raskolnikov)? The rough drafts testify to the difficulty the author experienced
in arriving at a suitable denouement. The "vision of Christ" and his
heroism at the fire had to be discarded; Svidrigailov, and not Raskolnikov fell heir to the solution of suicide. An exterior denouement still
remained: his giving himself up to the authorities, the trial, his deporta-
tion to the penal colony; but this did not suffice for an interior, spiritual
denouement. Raskolnikov did not repent and did not "rise" again to a
new life. There is only a promise of his resurrection in the concluding
words of the epilogue: the criminal is still young; the miracle-working
force of life will sustain him. This "philosophy of life" which in the
novel is expressed by Porfiry Petrovich had already been indicated in the
rough drafts. "But now it's life that I want; [I thirst for] life and I will
live," exclaims the murderer. "Suddenly morose desolation and infinite
pride and the struggle that life might not completely perish, but *that
there will be life*." After much hesitation the author finally arrived at this
compromise as a solution. The murderer has not yet been saved, but he
can be saved if he will completely give himself up to a spontaneous, irrational love of life. Naturally this is not yet faith; it is only the way to
it. Dostoevsky wrote down his thoughts on the meaning of suffering. "The
idea of the novel, the Orthodox outlook: in what does Orthodoxy lie.[3]
There is no happiness in comfort; happiness is purchased at the price of
suffering. . . . Man is not born for happiness. Man earns happiness, and
this always through suffering. There is no injustice here, for the *calling
and consciousness of life* are arrived at by experience pro and contra and
one must draw this experience upon one's self (by suffering, such is the
law of our planet); but this immediate consciousness, which is felt as a
living process, is a joy of such great intensity that one can pay for it by
years of suffering." This concept of suffering as the source of consciousness had already been expressed in *Notes from Underground*. Suffering is
the law of our planet. The man who accepts life, of his own will chooses
suffering and in this "calling of life" he realizes intense joy. Raskolnikov
is too immersed in life to perish from his demonic idea. By the whole
"living process" he is bound to life's mystical force. The denouement of
Crime and Punishment is founded upon this idea. It is interesting that
the author considered it an "Orthodox outlook."

[3] [In his notebooks, Dostoevsky often put down his thoughts in short, incomplete
sentences.–ED.]

The First Sentence in *Crime and Punishment*, the Word "Crime," and Other Matters

by Vadim V. Kozhinov

Early one evening, during an exceptional heat wave in the beginning of July, a young man walked out into the street from the little room he rented from tenants on S. Place, and slowly, almost irresolutely, set off in the direction of K. Bridge. (I, 1)

At first glance this sentence appears to be no more than a dry communiqué: "information." It seems that we are being informed only of the time and place of the action, the hero's age (he is a young man), his general status (he rents a little room from tenants), etc.; but in authentic, great art there are no details which serve purely informational purposes. First of all, this external, almost ritually "informational" feature of the novel's first sentence has . . . considerable artistic meaning. The accent on precision and authenticity in the opening sentence, its almost documentary character (and, in particular, the masking of place names) has its own special aesthetic impact. Moreover, every detail in a real work of art is linked organically with the whole. This first sentence, indeed, represents the embryo of the whole huge novel.

Take, for example, one word: the hero sets out "slowly, almost *irresolutely*." The word "irresolution" [*nereshimost'*] and the various word formations from the same root come up repeatedly in the novel, especially in the final scenes (for example, "resolution," "solution" [*razreshenie*]; "insoluble" [*nerazreshimo*]; "inability to make up one's mind" [*ne reshat'sja*]; "indecisively" [*nereshitel'no*]; "decided" [*resheno*]; "undecided" [*nereshennoe*]; "decision" [*reshenie*]—the final one). But we need not go very far into the novel: in the middle of the first chapter we find the same word again: "and in spite of all the mocking monologues about his own impotence and *irresolution*" etc. A little further on, as Raskolnikov

"*The First Sentence in* Crime and Punishment, *the Word 'Crime,' and Other Matters*" [*Editor's title*], by Vadim V. Kozhinov. *Excerpts from an essay*, "Prestuplenie i nakazanie F. M. Dostoevskogo" ["*F. M. Dostoevsky's* Crime and Punishment"] *in* Tri shedevra russkoj klassiki [Three Masterpieces of Russian Classics] (*Moscow, 1971*), *pp. 118–129; 144–151. Translated from the Russian by Robert Louis Jackson.*

ruminates over the letter he has received from his mother: "It was clear
that he should no longer be moping, suffering passively, brooding over
the problem's being *insoluble*; he ought to be doing something right away,
immediately, as soon as possible. Come what may he had to *decide* on
something, anything, or—" (I, 4) And then the scene in the restaurant
(I, 6) where Raskolnikov overhears the arguments of some student and the
reply of an officer: "Well, if you want to know what I think, I think if
you wouldn't *decide* to do it yourself, then there's no question of justice
here!" etc. etc.

We are dealing here with one of the key words of the novel, one which
speaks directly to its content, expresses its full meaning. *Crime and Punishment* is a novel about *insoluble* situations and *fateful decisions* that
have tragic consequences. Dmitry Pisarev[1] pointed this out long ago in
one of the first critical studies of the novel, "Struggle for Life" (*Bor'ba
za zhizn'*, 1867). Pisarev points out that the circumstances of Sonia
Marmeladov—circumstances in which she is obliged to make a "choice"
—are such as to render

> inapplicable the rules and precepts which govern moral behavior in every-
> day life; precise observance of any of these rules will lead a person right
> into the absurd. . . . Even the detached observer, pondering so extraor-
> dinary a situation, will become baffled and think that he has landed in
> some new, quite fantastic world where everything is topsy-turvy and where
> our usual notions of good and evil no longer seem to have any binding
> force. What would you say, indeed, about the behavior of Sofya Sem-
> yonovna? . . . Which voice should this girl heed as the voice of conscience:
> the one which advises her to "sit at home and endure, die from hunger
> along with your father, mother, brother and sisters, but preserve your moral
> purity to the end"? or the voice that says: "do not spare yourself, do not
> protect yourself, but give of everything you have, sell yourself, disgrace
> and pollute yourself, but at all costs rescue, console, support those people,
> feed and comfort them if only for a week"? I very much envy those of my
> readers who have the ability or knowledge to resolve such questions readily,
> forthrightly and without hesitation. I myself must confess that I am baffled
> in the face of such questions: conflicting views and arguments present
> themselves; my thoughts get tangled and confused; I lose my way and
> flounder in my analysis.

One should note that the man who expresses these thoughts is the kind
of person who as a rule inclines toward rectilinear, narrow and dogmatic
judgments and opinions. . . . But in this instance he quite correctly per-

---

[1] Dmitry I. Pisarev (1840–1868), Russian essayist and critic, a materialist and socialist;
in his long review of Dostoevsky's novel he argued that poverty was the underlying
"causal motive" for Raskolnikov's crime. "The crime was committed not because
Raskolnikov, in bouts of philosophizing, convinced himself of its lawfulness, ration-
ality, and necessity. On the contrary, Raskolnikov began to philosophize to this effect
and convince himself only because circumstances drove him to crime." [ED.]

ceived the unique character of the artistic "situations" in Dostoevsky's novel. Many years later, the well-known scholar V. F. Pereverzev[2] observed that for Raskolnikov life is "a tragic clash between self-will and humiliation," necessitates choosing between the role of aggressor or victim; the hero, "helplessly struggling to resolve this social contradiction, at one moment embraces the principle of self-will; at another, reverently, and even passionately he bows before humility and submission." Dostoevsky, of course, well understood the unique character of his novel. Even in his first formulation of the idea of *Crime and Punishment* he stresses that his hero is confronted with "insoluble questions." [3] . . .

"During an exceptional heat wave": This is not a mere weather report. . . . The whole novel takes place in an atmosphere of unbearable and suffocating heat and stench: the hero is staggered by it to the point of fainting; it is not only the atmosphere of a city in July, but the *atmosphere of crime.*

The little room which resembles, we later learn, a closet and a tomb, appears throughout the novel as a vital artistic device illuminating the action and meaning of the work. Even the rather matter-of-fact notation that Raskolnikov "rented from tenants" is very important. It points to the extreme *instability and rootlessness* of Raskolnikov. . . . Sonia Marmeladov, too, rents a room "from tenants"; "I didn't know that you too lived off tenants," she observes when she visits Raskolnikov. . . .

Let us take another word which often appears in the novel: "yellow" [*zheltyj*]. It might be called the novel's basic "color." The apartment of the old moneylender has "yellow wallpaper," furniture of "yellow wood," paintings which appear in "yellow frames." She herself is wearing a "yellowish jacket." Even in the dream in which Raskolnikov goes through the motions of repeating the murder his eye is caught by the "yellow sofa" in the old woman's room. Raskolnikov's little room is lined with "filthy yellow" wallpaper, and when he faints in the police station, they hand him "a yellow glass filled with yellow water." As a result of his illness Raskolnikov's face turns "pale yellow." Even Marmeladov has a "yellow face." Again, we find "yellowish" wallpaper in Sonia's room. The furniture in Porfiry Petrovich's office is made of "yellow wood," while the face of the inspector is "dark yellow." The woman who throws herself into the canal in the presence of Raskolnikov has a "yellow" face. The little houses on Petrovsky island are "bright yellow." The list could be extended, but it should be noted, too, that as a rule very few colors are to be found in the novel, and of these only yellow is used more than a few times. The predominance of this color is hardly accidental . . . and

[2] Valerian F. Pereverzev (1882–1968), author of *Tvorchestvo Dostoevskogo* [*Dostoevsky's Creative Work*] (1912), the first major attempt to analyze Dostoevsky's work from a Marxist sociological point of view. [ED.]

[3] See Dostoevsky's letter to Katkov, in this collection, pp. 9–10. [ED.]

points to a role both complex and varied. In one striking scene, a few days after the murder, Raskolnikov revisits the old woman's flat and comes across some workmen:

> They were papering the walls with new wallpaper, white with lilac flowers, replacing the dirty, yellow old one. Somehow this displeased Raskolnikov terribly. He regarded the new wallpaper with hostility, as though he resented the change. (II, 6)

Why was he so displeased? True, Raskolnikov would tend to react negatively to any alteration of the scene where he has experienced one of the most fateful moments of his life; but the mention here of a change in wallpaper from yellow to white is, obviously, not fortuitous. Yellow clearly is the color of that world where the crime was conceived (Raskolnikov's little room is also yellow) and where it was executed.

That is not all. The color yellow characterizes Raskolnikov's inner world as well. There is a significant juxtaposition of two words in the novel: the word "yellow" [*zheltyj*—pronounced *zholtyj*] frequently is found in proximity with another word of the same root: "bilious," or "jaundiced" [*zhelchnyj*—pronounced *zholchnyj*]. This word also occurs often in the novel. Thus, we read about Raskolnikov:

> A heavy, bilious [*zhelchnyj*], angry smile played around his lips. He lay back his head on his meager and bedraggled pillow, and he thought. He thought for a long time. . . . At last he felt it grow close and stuffy in that little yellow [*zheltyj*] room." (I, 3) . . .

The juxtaposition of "*zhelchnyj*" and "*zheltyj*," bilious and yellow, basically involves an interplay of internal and external elements, the way the hero responds to the world and the world itself. The rich and dramatic meanings that accrue to the word "yellow" clearly relate to that interplay. Other meanings, to be sure, also are grafted upon the word "yellow." Thus, Sonia, who lives in a "yellow" room, also—as we are reminded frequently in the novel—lives "by the yellow ticket." [4] This painful allusion to prostitution is part of the general meaning of the word "yellow." . . .

Finally, the word "yellow" suggests that *Crime and Punishment* is quite entirely a *Petersburg* novel, indeed the image of Petersburg in Russian literature is closely associated with the color yellow. . . . Probably, too, the abundance of "yellow" in Dostoevsky's novel relates to the general coloration of the city. But when all is said and done the atmosphere of the novel itself, that interplay of "biliousness" and "yellowness," have deeper significance; we are not dealing with a word in the ordinary sense, but with an element of the artistic world of *Crime and Punishment*. . . .

The word "crime" [*prestuplenie*] and its variants continually crop up in

---

[4] The "yellow ticket" refers to the identification papers, on yellow paper, carried by prostitutes in prerevolutionary times. [ED.]

the novel.[5] Thus, Raskolnikov says to Sonia, who has sacrificed herself for the sake of her family: "You, too, have *transgressed [perestupila]* . . . you found within yourself you were able to transgress . . . you took a life . . . *your own* (what's the difference!)." We read, of Raskolnikov's mother, that she "could consent to much . . . but there was always a line . . . beyond which no circumstance could compel her to step *[perestupit']*." At the very beginning of the novel, Marmeladov tells Raskolnikov how he "transgressed." . . . Right after his meeting with Marmeladov, Raskolnikov receives a letter from his mother in which once again the theme of the "criminality" of man occupies the foreground, in which the mother blesses her daughter for sacrificing herself for the sake of her brother, because she, Dunia, "can endure much" (although even for Dunia, as for her mother, there exists a "line" beyond which she will not step). Finally, the *criminal* image of Svidrigailov emerges in the letter.

The theme of "transgression" *[perestupanije]* ever broadens and deepens: Marmeladov who "sins against" his wife and Sonia; Sonia who "sins against" herself; then Dunia ready to "sin against" herself;[6] and finally Svidrigailov, who knows no "boundaries." At last, after the story of Marmeladov and the letter from his mother, Raskolnikov encounters Sonia's "double"—a drunken girl on the boulevard who is being pursued by a man whom Raskolnikov there and then christens "Svidrigailov." Raskolnikov tries to help the girl, but his cup is already running over, and he maliciously cries out: "Well, let them devour each other alive. What do I care?" Raskolnikov's crime is committed in this "criminal" world.

As Raskolnikov contemplates killing the rich old lady we read that he "decided . . . that what he contemplated doing was 'not a crime'." Here is a complex "game" with a word; of course, not some playful distraction, but a tragic "game" with serious consequences. Raskolnikov is right in the sense that his act, examined in terms of its motives and goals, goes far beyond a strictly juridical framework. Superficially viewed, one might even suppose that Raskolnikov murders the rich old lady in order to find the means to finish his education and help his family. He would even seem to have some distant plans: to be of some use to mankind later on, to be "philanthropic" at the expense of an evil and useless old woman.

[5] The Russian word *"prestuplenie,"* which means literally "overstepping" or "going over, across," is generally translated as "crime" (from the Latin *crimen*—verdict, judicial decision, that which is subject to such a decision). In contemporary use the term "crime" tends to be applied simply to actions which are contrary to the laws of the state, that is, it is primarily *legal* in meaning. The English word "transgression" (from the Latin *transgressio*—a going across, going over, transgression of the law), though without legal usage, conveys in full the idea of moral violation of human or divine law. The Russian word *prestuplenie* conveys the Biblical sense of moral violation or "overstepping" the Law, while at the same time, like "crime," it serves to define actions contrary to the laws of the state. [ED.]

[6] Variants of the Russian verb *"perestupit' "* (to step over, transgress) are used here. [ED.]

However, Raskolnikov did not make use of the stolen valuables (indeed, he does not even take stock of what he had taken); as we later learn, he even *knew beforehand* that he would make no use of them.

In short, viewed in the light of its deep inner motives, Raskolnikov's deed is not a crime in a juridical sense which always involves the implied question: who gains from the crime, and why? He commits the crime not out of any desire for gain, not because he is evil and cruel by nature, and not even for the purpose of "revenging" himself on society; yet Raskolnikov's deed is a *crime* in the most profound and radical sense. He says to Sonia: "If only I had killed because I was hungry—how *happy* I would have been now!" Yes, his deed is more terrible than any ordinary crime because he not only killed, but he wanted to affirm the *right* to murder, to affirm the very right to crime.

Another aspect of the novel's action must be considered here: it is not only the old moneylender whom Raskolnikov kills. He also brings his ax down on her sister, Lizaveta—a meek and downtrodden creature, gentle and humble, that same Lizaveta who but recently mended his shirt. She was a friend of Sonia's, even resembled her. When Raskolnikov confesses his crime to Sonia, he "suddenly saw the face of Lizaveta in her face." Killing Lizaveta was clearly almost the same as killing Sonia. Raskolnikov himself exclaims: "Lizaveta! Sonia! Poor creatures, meek, with meek eyes . . . Dear ones! . . . They give everything away . . . they look out meekly and gently." (III, 6)

These remarks about the person he has just murdered cannot be taken as cynicism; yet the murder of Lizaveta would appear to be far more terrible than the murder of a wicked and despotic old moneygrubber. One might note, in passing, that in an early version of the novel the gravity of Raskolnikov's crime is underscored by the fact that Lizaveta is pregnant: "There was an autopsy. She had been six months' pregnant. A boy. Dead," remarks the cook Nastasia in that version. . . .

"Poor Lizaveta," reflects Raskolnikov. "Why did she turn up at this point? But it's strange, all the same, that I hardly think about her, almost as though I hadn't even killed her." He explains to Sonia that he had killed Lizaveta "accidentally." In fact, Raskolnikov did kill Lizaveta in a state of extreme confusion, almost madness; it seemed as if he acted almost in self-defense. Yet he killed the old lady quite deliberately, and for the sake of affirming the right to murder. It was a kind of murdering of *man in general,* after which a person can murder anyone and everyone he pleases. Weighed with this crime the "accidental" murder of Lizaveta is indeed scarcely even a crime, rather the wild act of an unbalanced man who cannot be held accountable.

The death of Lizaveta, of course, in a dramatic way underscores the terrible meaning of Raskolnikov's deed: once he has yielded to his "theory," he is almost compelled to kill even somebody whom he had not wanted to kill; his crime, one might say, sets off a chain reaction. Nonetheless, the murder of Lizaveta primarily serves to focus attention on the grave import of the murder of the old moneylender. . . .

We note in *Crime and Punishment* a tight interplay and struggle between consciousness, "idea," on the one hand, and a direct, integral relation to life on the other—what Dostoevsky himself in his notes to the novel defined as "something directly felt by the body and spirit, i.e., the whole living process." For this very reason, it is a mistake to view the novel as a sort of "philosophical" work whose whole essence consists in the development and clash of ideas. When we attend only to the movement of ideas we artificially isolate one part of the novel, a part which loses its real meaning when divorced from the rest. The whole build-up to the murder, for example, is not simply the maturation of an idea, but its constant interplay with the whole "living process," Raskolnikov's confrontation with people, facts, objects (here the "encounters" of the hero with Petersburg, its houses, taverns, streets, bridges, canals, play a special role). The motive force in the novel is not an idea, but thinking man.

It is not enough to speak of the interaction of idea with the whole "living process"; the very life of ideas as such in the novel is unique. To perceive the ideological plan of *Crime and Punishment* only as the development of thought—complex and multidimensional as these thoughts may be—is still to grasp nothing of that structure which embodies the inner essence of the work.

M. M. Bakhtin has brilliantly analyzed the unique life of ideas in *Crime and Punishment*.[7] We may cite his discussion of Raskolnikov's first interior monologue; the hero's "idea" is encountered for the first time in all its magnitude. Raskolnikov has just met Marmeladov and learned the story of Sonia; he has already received the letter from his mother, where he learns also about Dunia's projected marriage to Luzhin, and of his mother's belief that this marriage might turn out to be helpful to him. The hero ponders all this:

> It is clear that the number one attraction on the stage here is none other than Rodion Romanovich Raskolnikov. Well, why not? She can make him happy, support him at the university, make him a partner in a law firm. . . . And his mother? Well, never mind. Have a look at Rodia, though—precious Rodia, the firstborn! . . . Indeed, we would even go the way of Sonia! . . . But this sacrifice, this sacrifice, have you taken the measure of your sacrifice, both of you? You have? . . . Do you realize, Dunia dear, that little Sonia's lot is not in any way more squalid than life with Mr. Luzhin? . . . What in the world did you take me for? I don't want your sacrifice; I don't want it, mother dear! As long as I live it shall not come to that! It shall not, shall not come to that! I refuse to accept it!" Suddenly he recollected himself, and paused. "Shall not? What can you do to prevent

[7] M. M. Bakhtin (b. 1895), important Russian scholar, author of *Problemy poetiki Dostoevskogo* (Leningrad, 1929; revised and enlarged in 1963), a study of the polyphonic character of Dostoevsky's novels and other stylistic questions. Kozhinov's essay is dedicated to Bakhtin. [ED.]

it? Forbid it? By what right? What can you promise in return to claim such
a right?" . . . He had to come to a decision at all costs, or else—"Or renounce life altogether!" he cried out in a frenzy. . . . "Do you understand,
my dear sir, do you understand what it means when you have nowhere to
go?" Suddenly he remembered Marmeladov's question of yesterday. "For
every man needs to have at least somewhere he can go." (I, 4)

All these individuals—the mother, Dunia, Luzhin, Marmeladov and
Sonia—are "reflected," writes M. M. Bakhtin, "in Raskolnikov's consciousness (with all their 'truths,' with all their points of view); all of
them have entered into his interior monologue which throughout takes
the form of dialogue; and it is a vigorous and deadly earnest dialogue in
which Raskolnikov engages them, one involving the most fateful questions and decisions of life. . . . Raskolnikov's interior monologue is a
splendid example of the micro-dialogue: every line in it is two-voiced:
voices dispute in every one. . . . At the beginning of the above passage
Raskolnikov evokes Dunia's speech with her own morally decisive and
convincing tone; he grafts onto these lines his own ironic, indignant expression, so that the reader hears two voices at the same time: that of
Raskolnikov and that of Dunia. Further on ('Well never mind. Have a
look at Rodia, though' etc.) he hears the mother's voice filled with love
and tenderness and yet at the same time Raskolnikov's voice echoes with
its bitter irony, indignation (over the sacrifice) and yet melancholy re-
sponding love. The voices of Sonia and Marmeladov also create overtones
to the words of Raskolnikov. Dialogue penetrates every line of the passage
and wakes in it both struggle and emotion." [8]

This "dialogue" structure permeates the narration in the entire novel.
The voices of the heroes, writes Bakhtin, "continually listen to one another, echo one another. . . . Not a single act, not a single essential
idea of the main heroes takes shape apart from this dialogue of 'battling
truths.' " [9]

It is obvious that dialogue in the usual sense occupies a large part of
Crime and Punishment. Raskolnikov argues intensively with Sonia,
Svidrigailov, Luzhin, Dunia and Razumikhin. His dialogue-battles with
the court investigator Porfiry Petrovich have a very special character. But
these direct, open dialogues only reveal the real nature of the novel as a
whole, for in the final analysis, the whole novel is one continuous dialogue. Everything that is reflected in the inner world of Raskolnikov
takes on the "form of a passionate dialogue with missing interlocutors.
. . . And it is in this dialogue that he strives to 'resolve his thought.' . . .
By this means, Raskolnikov's idea emerges in all its limitations, nuances,
possibilities, in all its diverse interrelations with other important points
of view. As it loses its character of monologue, its insularity as abstraction
and theory . . . the idea takes on the contradictory complexity and

[8] M. Bakhtin, *Problemy poetiki Dostoevskogo* (Moscow, 1963), pp. 100–101.
[9] Ibid.

protean character of a seminal idea which comes into being, lives and acts in the great dialogue of the epoch and converses with kindred ideas of other epochs." [10] . . .

The development of ideas—or rather the uninterrupted dialogue of ideas—emerges in *Crime and Punishment* as a kind of living organism, that is, it has its own *artistic* nature. Philosophical ideas are embodied in real imagery, are inseparable from the images of people, just as events, acts, experiences and desires are real. Raskolnikov's "philosophical" disputes with Sonia, Razumikhin, Svidrigailov, Porfiry Petrovich and other heroes are authentic dramatic scenes of real artistic content.

[10] Ibid., pp. 117–18.

Philosophical Pro and Contra in Part One

of *Crime and Punishment*

by *Robert Louis Jackson*

I suffered these deeds more than I acted them.

Oedipus

The burden of Part One is the dialectic of consciousness in Raskolnikov. This dialectic propels him to crime and, in so doing, uncovers for the reader the "motives" leading him to crime: motives deeply rooted in his character and in his efforts to come to terms with the necessities of his existence. Leo Tolstoy grasped the essence of the matter when he wrote that Raskolnikov lived his "true life" when he was

> lying on the sofa in his room, deliberating not at all about the old woman, nor even as to whether it is or is not permissible at the will of one man to wipe from the face of the earth another, unnecessary and harmful person, but whether he ought to live in St. Petersburg or not, whether he ought to accept money from his mother or not, and on other questions not at all relating to the old woman. And then at that time—in that region—quite independent of animal activities—the question of whether he would or not kill the old woman was decided. ("Why Men Stupefy Themselves," 1890)

But if the fundamental matters or issues over which Raskolnikov deliberates are very immediate and practical ones, his responses to these matters have broad implications that have direct bearing on the crime. Here we may rightly speak of a moral-philosophical pro and contra.

Part One begins with a "test" visit (*proba*) to the old pawnbroker and ends with a visit-for-real in which Raskolnikov murders the old lady and, incidentally, her sister Lizaveta. The murder itself is also, in a deeper sense, a "test" or experiment to determine whether he has the "right" to transgress. Raskolnikov starts out in a state of indecision or irresolution (I, 1) and ends with a decisive action—murder (I, 7): an apparent resolution of his initial indecision. But does the murder really constitute a

"Philosophical Pro and Contra in Part One of Crime and Punishment," *by Robert Louis Jackson. Copyright* © *1973 by Prentice-Hall, Inc. This essay appears for the first time in this volume.*

resolution of Raskolnikov's dialectic? Does he really "decide" to murder
the pawnbroker? Or does not "chance," rather, serve to mask his failure
to decide with his whole being? Is he master or slave here? The final line
alone of Part One suggests the answer: "Fragments and shreds of thoughts
swarmed in his head; but he could not get hold of a single one, he could
not dwell on a single one, in spite of all his trying." (I, 7) Raskolnikov's
dialectic of consciousness continues to be dramatized in his thoughts,
actions and relationships after the murder (Parts II–VI). It is only in the
epilogue (chap. 2) that this dialectic is dissolved—not resolved—on a
new, developing plane of consciousness.[1]

The movement from test to test, from rehearsal to experimental crime,
from theory to practice, is marked by a constant struggle and debate on all
levels of Raskolnikov's consciousness. Each episode—the meeting with
Marmeladov and his family (chap. 2), Raskolnikov's reading of his
mother's letter with its account of family affairs (chap. 3), his encounter
with the violated girl and the policeman (chap. 4) and his dream of the
beating of the mare (chap. 5)—is marked by a double movement: a motion of sympathy and a motion of disgust, of attraction and recoil; each
episode attests to what one critic has called Raskolnikov's "moral maximalism";[2] yet each attests to a deepening scepticism and despair on the
part of Raskolnikov, a tragic tension toward crime in both a psychological
and philosophical sense.[3]

The immediate issues of this pro and contra are nothing more or less
than injustice and human suffering and the question of how one shall
respond to them. But the deeper evolving question—on which turns
Raskolnikov's ultimate response to injustice and suffering—is a judgment
of man and his world: is he a morally viable creature or simply and ir-
redeemably bad? Do man and the world make sense?[4] Raskolnikov's
murder of the old pawnbroker is the final expression of the movement of
his dialectic toward a tragic judgment of man and society. The ideological
concomitant of his paralysis of moral will (the scenes following his chance
encounter on the street with Lizaveta) is a rationalistic humanism that is
unable to come to terms with evil in human existence; lacking larger
spiritual dimensions, this ideology ends by postulating incoherence and

---

[1] Raskolnikov's inability to focus his thoughts on anything, his inability consciously to
"resolve" anything after his reconciliation with Sonia in the epilogue ("he was simply
feeling") constitutes, of course, a qualitatively different state of consciousness from the
chaos of mind experienced right after the murder. The almost symmetrical opposition
of these two "moments" of consciousness is not accidental; the movement or shift from
one to the other constitutes the movement in Raskolnikov's consciousness from hate
(unfreedom) to love (freedom).

[2] See N. M. Chirkov's essay in this collection, pp. 49–70.

[3] In turn, Raskolnikov's internal conflict in Parts II–VI may be regarded as a reverse
movement, a tension toward redemption.

[4] These questions, of course, are explicit in *The Brothers Karamazov.*

Raskolnikov's view of fate

chaos in man and his environment and, in turn, a universe in which man is a victim of "fate."

The stark realism and pathos of Marmeladov's person and family at first cools the hot and agitated Raskolnikov. The novel rises to its first epiphany in the tavern: out of the troubled posturing and grotesquerie of Marmeladov comes a mighty prose poem of love, compassion, and forgiveness (echoing Luke 7, 36–50); it constitutes an antithesis to Raskolnikov's proud and rebellious anger. Raskolnikov visits the Marmeladovs, responds warmly to them, and leaves some money behind. But the same scene, focusing on the hopelessness and tragedy of Raskolnikov's environment, evokes finally incredulity and despair in him. If Marmeladov's "confession," which opens chapter 2, accents the central redemptive notes in *Crime and Punishment,* the final lines of the chapter stress antithetical notes of despair and damnation. The sight of human degradation is so overwhelming as to evoke in Raskolnikov fundamental doubts about man and human nature. Stunned that people can live in this way, that indignity, vulgarity and discord can become an accepted part of one's life, Raskolnikov explodes: "Man can get used to anything—the scoundrel [*podlets*]!" These strange ruminations follow: "But what if man really isn't a *scoundrel,* man in general, I mean, the whole human race; if he is not, that means that all the rest is prejudice, just imaginary fears, and there are no barriers, and that is as it should be!" (I, 2) These lines are crucial in posing the underlying moral and philosophical issues of *Crime and Punishment.*

The motif of "adaptation" is heard throughout Dostoevsky's works—from *Poor Folk* (1846) through *Notes from the House of the Dead* (1860–61) to *The Brothers Karamazov* (1881). It attests, from one point of view, to human endurance, the will to survive; yet from another view, it is a deeply tragic idea, implying that man will yield feebly to suffering, oppression, injustice, unfreedom, in short, to triumphant evil. Man in this conception is man as the Grand Inquisitor finds him: weak and vile. Such adaptation arouses only contempt in the rebellious Raskolnikov. His rebellion, of course, implies a positive standard or norm of human behavior, morality, life. Merely to speak of man as a "scoundrel" for adapting to evil is to posit another ideal, to affirm, by implication, that man ought not to yield weakly to degradation and evil. But the thought that occurs to Raskolnikov at this point is one which links him directly with the Grand Inquisitor. We may paraphrase his thought as follows: what if all this vile adaptation to evil is *not* a deviation from a norm; that is, what if villainy pure and simple is, *ab ovo,* the human condition? What if—as Raskolnikov later puts it—everyone of the people scurrying about on the streets "is a scoundrel and predator by his very nature"? (VI, 7) If such be the case, if man is truly defective by nature, then all our moral systems, standards, injunctions, pejorative epithets (the very word "scoundrel") are senseless "prejudices," "imaginary fears"; it follows that if human nature is, morally speaking, an empty plain, then "there can be no barriers," all is permissible, "and that is as it should be!" [5]

Svidrigailov, the character who comes closest to a complete embodiment of the principle that "all is permissible," also poses the question that Raskolnikov is deliberating, though more dispassionately and cynically. Defending himself against the charges that he persecuted Dunia in his home, he observes:

> Just suppose, however, that I, too, am a man, *et nihil humanum* . . . in a word, that I can be attracted and fall in love (and of course that doesn't happen to us according to our own will), then everything's accounted for in the most natural manner. The whole question boils down to this: am I a monster or am I a victim? Well, and what if I am a victim? (IV, 1)

Barely concealed in Svidrigailov's jocular question, of course, is the issue of human nature, the character of man. The underlying ethical and finally philosophical import of his question—"Am I a monster or am I myself a victim?"—is clear: does a consideration of my acts—man's acts ("Just suppose . . . that I, too, am a man") fall under the rubric of ethics or the laws of nature? Are we really responsible for our behavior? Is the morally pejorative epithet "monster" (or "scoundrel") really in order? Are we not simply creatures of "nature"? Svidrigailov, one notes, likes to appeal to "natural" tendencies; very much like the Marquis de Sade's alter ego Clément (*Justine*, 1791) or Dolmance (*La philosophie dans le boudoir*, 1795), he appeals to "nature" as a reason for disposing entirely of moral categories or judgment. "In this debauchery, at least, there is something constant, based even on nature, and not subject to fantasy," Svidrigailov remarks in his last conversation with Raskolnikov.[6] (VI, 3)

---

[5] Raskolnikov's intense moral concerns provide evidence, of course, that man is not "a scoundrel and predator" by nature. And it is, finally, the idea of adaptation as testimony to man's endurance and will to live that is ultimately accepted by Raskolnikov. Thus, Raskolnikov, after an encounter with prostitutes on the streets, declares that it would be better to live an eternity on a "square yard of space" than to die. "To live and to live and to live and to live! How true that is! God, how true! What a scoundrel man is! *And he's a scoundrel who calls him a scoundrel for that,*" he added a minute later. (II, 6) My italics.

[6] His cruel tastes, Clément argues in *Justine*, are given to him by "Nature." "Oh, Thérèse, is there any crime here? Is this the name to designate what serves Nature? Is it in man's power to commit crimes?" Nature's "primary and most imperious inspirations" enjoin man "to pursue his happiness at no matter whose expense. The doctrine of brotherly love is a fiction we owe to Christianity and not to Nature." "But the man you describe is a monster," Thérèse protests, while Clément rejoins: "The man I describe is in tune with Nature." "He is a savage beast," insists Thérèse. And Clément retorts: "Why, is not the tiger or the leopard, of whom this man is, if you wish, a replica, like man created by Nature and created to prosecute Nature's intentions?" (Cf. The Marquis de Sade, *Justine* [New York: Grove Press, 1965], pp. 607–8.) From the sensualist-philosopher de Sade to the philosopher-sensualist Svidrigailov is no step at all. In his novels, particularly in *The Brothers Karamazov*, Dostoevsky comes to grips with the thoughts expressed here (the question of whether Dostoevsky actually read de Sade is beside the point, though references to de Sade in his works, especially in

Indeed, Svidrigailov's conception of man would appear to be wholly biological—"Now I pin all my hope on anatomy alone, by God!" (IV, 1) —a point of view that certainly undercuts any concept of personal responsibility or free will. The concept *"homo sum, et nihil humanum a me alienum puto"* ("I am a man and nothing human is alien to me") was for Dostoevsky a profoundly *moral* concept, implying the obligation squarely to confront human reality. "Man on the surface of the earth does not have the right to turn away and ignore what is taking place on earth," he wrote in a letter in 1871, "and there are lofty moral reasons for this: *homo sum et nihil humanum,* etc." Svidrigailov, of course, takes the concept as an apologia for doing whatever one pleases. To be a man, in his view, is to be open to all that is in nature, that is, to nature in himself; it is to be in the power of nature (if not to *be* nature) and, therefore, not to be responsible. We have noted that he pins his hopes on "anatomy." But his hopes for salvation through Dunia, and his final suicide, are evidence that his confidence in anatomy has its cracks and fissures. In the final analysis, then, even for Svidrigailov (though infinitely more so for Raskolnikov), the concept "monster or victim?"—morally responsible or free to commit all vilenesses?—is a fateful *question;* precisely this fact, in Dostoevsky's view, distinguishes man, even the Svidrigailovs, from de Sade's tigers and leopards.

The problem raised by Raskolnikov and Svidrigailov, and lived out in their life dramas, is posed directly by Ivan Karamazov. Apropos of his belief that man is incapable of Christian love, Ivan observes: "The real issue is whether all this comes from people's bad qualities or simply because it is their nature." Raskolnikov's pessimistic conjecture at the conclusion of chapter 2 (and, even more, the evidence of his dream in chapter 5) can be compared with Ivan's bitter judgment of man in his famous "rebellion." It can be described as the opening, and dominant motif, in a prelude to murder. The whole of *Crime and Punishment* is an effort to refute this judgment of man, to provide an answer, through Raskolnikov himself, to his own tragic conjecture. The action in Part One, however, is "moved" by the almost syllogistic logic of Raskolnikov's pessimistic conjecture.

Chapter 2, then, contains the extreme moral and philosophical polarities of the novel: affirmation of the principle of love, compassion and freedom (which will ultimately embrace Raskolnikov through Sonia) and the principle of hate, a pessimistic view of man as a "scoundrel" by

---

Notes from the House of the Dead suggest familiarity with his work). Dostoevsky's own point of view, though antithetical to de Sade's in the final analysis, is complex and, like everything else in his thought, antinomian. What is certain, however, is that for him the Christian doctrine of brotherly love is not a "fiction"; or, put in another way, this doctrine—in the face of what Dostoevsky fearfully detects in man's earthly sensual nature—is the most important "fiction" in human existence, without which, he insisted once in his notebooks, life on earth would be "senseless."

nature, and a projection of the idea that "all is permissible." The events of chapter 2 bring Raskolnikov full circle from compassion to nihilistic rage. Exposed is that realm of "underground," ambivalent consciousness where love is compounded of pain, and hate—of frustrated love; where extreme compassion for suffering and for the good are transmuted into a contempt for man; where that contempt, finally, signals despair with love and with the good and nourishes that urge for violence and sick craving for power that is born not only from an acute sense of injustice but from a tragic feeling of one's own real helplessness and irreversible humiliation. Here is our first contact with the matrix of Raskolnikov's "theoretical" crime, with the responses that will find explicit formulation in Raskolnikov's article and arguments. Here is the protean core of those shifting, seemingly contradictory "motives" (what Mochulsky has termed the "idea of Rastignac"—altruistic, utilitarian crime, and the "idea of Napoleon"—triumph over the "anthill," etc.[7]). Here we see how the raw material of social and psychological experience begins to generalize into social and philosophical "point of view"—ultimately, into those "ideas" of Raskolnikov that will tragically act back again upon life and experience.

The same cyclical pattern we have noted in chapter 2 dominates chapter 3. The chapter opens on a subtle note that disputes the depressing and abstract conjectures of Raskolnikov. Nastasia, the servant girl, brings him soup, chatters about food, about Raskolnikov's affairs. She is the epitome of a simplicity, warmth, and goodness that cannot be gainsaid. She is a kind of spiritual harbinger of Raskolnikov's mother, whose letter he receives. This letter, like the encounter with Marmeladov and his family, evokes a similar picture of self-sacrificing people who are helpless before the evil in the world, before the Luzhins and Svidrigailovs. Raskolnikov begins reading the letter with a kiss ("he quickly lifted it to his lips and kissed it") but ends it with "a heavy, bilious, angry smile" playing around his lips. The letter produces, finally, the same ugly sensations as the scene in the Marmeladov household, the same sympathy and compassion turning into rage and rebellion. Raskolnikov goes out for a walk as though "drunk": his shapeless body reflects his inner rage and distress. His initial defense of the violated girl (chap. 4) is followed almost immediately by a sense of "revulsion," a raging amoral anger. Starting out, then, with a gesture of goodness, Raskolnikov characteristically ends by abandoning the girl to evil in a classical gesture of "underground" malice.

During Raskolnikov's walk (the early part of chapter 4), the central philosophical motif on the nature of man—the area of his vacillations—emerges in his reflections on his mother, Dunia and their situation. He

---

[7] See Konstantin Mochulsky's discussion of Dostoevsky's search for "motives" in his essay in this collection.

comprehends their sacrifice for him as an ascent to Golgotha, but in bitterness casts his mother and sister among the innocents, those "Schilleresque 'beautiful souls'" who wave the truth away, would rather not
admit the vile truth about man. Dunia, like Sonia, Raskolnikov realizes,
is prepared to suppress her moral feelings for the one she loves, for him.
Raskolnikov almost venomously rejects the idea of such sacrifice, sale
of one's freedom, peace of mind and conscience. It is a rejection, of course,
of the Christian spirit of sacrifice. "Dear little Sonia, Sonia Marmeladov,
Sonia eternal, while the world lasts! But this sacrifice, this sacrifice, have
you taken the measure of your sacrifice, both of you? Have you really?
Do you have the strength? Will it be of any use? Is it wise and reasonable?"
Raskolnikov's choice of words is symptomatic of his ideological illness.

To the impulses of the heart he opposes, in his bitterness and despair,
utility, scales, self-interest. And, of course, here is rich soil for the cultiva-
tion of ideas of utilitarian crime (I, 6). The appeal of utilitarian ethics
emerges from a despairing sense of the *uselessness* of all human striving
for justice and truth, from a sense of the vileness of human nature, and
a conviction that "people won't change, and nobody can reform them, and
it's not worth the effort!" (V, 4)

Raskolnikov rightly understands that what he opposes and rejects (that
is, the principle of love and self-sacrifice) is "eternal"; he rejects it in part
out of despair with evil, but in part in the name of a false principle of
self-affirmation and "triumph over the whole anthill," a false principle of
"freedom." "And I know now, Sonia, that whoever is strong and self-
confident in mind and spirit is their master!" (V,4) "Understand me well,"
Dostoevsky wrote in *Winter Notes on Summer Impressions* (1863), "volun-
tary, fully conscious self-sacrifice, utterly free of outside constraint, sacrifice of one's whole self for the benefit of all, is in my opinion the sign of
the highest development of individuality, of its supreme power, its absolute self-mastery and its most complete freedom of its own will."
Raskolnikov's rejection of his family's spirit of self-sacrifice, at least in
part, reflects his own distance from Dostoevsky's concept of self-sacrifice
and, chiefly, from the ideal of authentic freedom that such a spirit of self-
sacrifice implies.

But Raskolnikov's powerful impulses to good and his high potential
for self-sacrifice are short-circuited by a sense of overwhelming injustice
and evil, of absurd imbalance in the "scales" of good and evil. In the
face of the world's misery, the rapacious Svidrigailovs and Luzhins, the
pitiful and loathesome spectacle of *man-adapting*, Raskolnikov rebels:
"I don't want your sacrifice, Dunia; I don't want it, mother dear! As long
as I live it shall not come to that! It shall not, shall not come to that! I
refuse to accept it!" (I, 4)

Dostoevsky uses the word "anguish" to express Raskolnikov's state of
mind. His rebellion, indeed, looks back on the revolt of the man from
the "underground" and forward to Ivan Karamazov's rebellion against

divine harmony (if it be based on the innocent suffering of children). Deeply responsive to human suffering, Ivan, in his indignation, returns to God his "ticket" to future harmony; yet this same humanitarian revolt, with its despair in a meaningful universe, leads him unconsciously to sanction the murder of his father. This same ethical paradox lies at the root of Raskolnikov's crime. Starting out with love and compassion for the "eternal" Sonias, for Dunia and his mother, Raskolnikov ends up with a rejection of love and sacrifice and with a rage at evil: a rage which itself becomes disfigured, evil. This rage, in its origins ethically motivated, deforms Raskolnikov and accentuates in him the elements of sick pride and self-will.

It is no accident that in this state of mind Raskolnikov's thought is led back to his projected crime. "It shall not come to that": he is "robbing" his family, he feels; but what can he do? The letter from his mother exposes his helplessness in a realm that is dear to him, drives him onto the path of action. Either action or renunciation of life: "humbly accept my fate as it is, once and for all, strangle everything I have within me, and give up every right I have to act, to live and to love!" Suddenly a thought flashes through his mind. This is the " 'monstrous' dream" (*bezobraznaja mechta*, I, 1) of his crime, but now no longer a dream or vision, but taking on "some new and terrifying form that he had not known before." This new and threatening form is revealed to him in his "terrible dream" (*strashnyj son*) in chapter 5: the beating and killing of the mare.

Raskolnikov's dream, echoing earlier incidents, situations, and emotional experience, is a psychological metaphor in which we may distinguish the various responses of Raskolnikov to his projected crime: his deep psychological complicity in, and yet moral recoil before, the crime. What has received less attention, however, is the way in which the underlying philosophical pro and contra is revealed in the separate elements of the dream (pastoral church and cemetery episode, tumultuous tavern and mare-beating scene); how the scene of the beating itself, this picture of Russian man and reality, raises the central and grave question of Part One: what is the nature of man? In its oppressive realism, and in the pessimism of its "commentary" on man, this dream yields only to the tale "Akulka's Husband" in *Notes from the House of the Dead*: at the center of that episode is the stupefied life of the Russian village, the persecution and murder of a peasant girl. The story is the nethermost level of Dostoevsky's "hell": here there is no light, only brutality, ignorance, absolute loss of control, and the violation of all that is sacred: beauty, human dignity, life.

The opening recollection in Raskolnikov's dream, though dominated by an atmosphere of impending evil, embodies Dostoevsky's pure aesthetic-religious ideal. Everything is sacred form, harmony, and reverence in the boy's first memory of the tranquil open landscape, the stone church with its green cupola, the icons, the simple rituals, the cemetery and, finally, the tombs of his grandmother and younger brother with their clear promise of resurrection. "He loved this church" and its atmosphere. In this, Raskolnikov's purified and almost completely submerged memory of sacred form, spirituality and beauty, there lies, without question, the seed of Raskolnikov's own moral and spiritual renewal. But the path to the church and cemetery—to resurrection—goes by the tavern on the edge of town, with its crowd of drunken, brawling peasants with their "drunken, fearsome distorted faces," their "shapeless and hoarse singing." Here, everything is desecration and deformation. The faces of the people in Raskolnikov's nightmare tell the tale: this is a demonized universe.[8] It all created an "unpleasant impression" on the boy. On the deepest level of the dream, then, we may speak of the coexistence—passive, we shall see—of two barely contiguous worlds: the ideal world of Christianity, with its aesthetic-religious ideals, and the real world claimed by the devil.

But now again, as Raskolnikov dreams, it is a holiday, a day of religious observance; the peasants, however, are drunk and in riotous spirits. There is an overloaded cart drawn by a poor mare. Then, suddenly, a drunken crowd of peasants, shouting and singing, emerge from the tavern, "blind drunk, in red and blue shirts." At the invitation of the driver, Mikolka, they pile onto the cart, followed by a "fat, red-faced peasant woman" in a "red calico dress . . . plumed and beaded . . . she was cracking nuts and laughing. In the crowd all around they're laughing, too." Then, the effort to start the cart and the brutal process of beating, and finally killing, the mare commences. This terrible and terrifying scene is simultaneously a rehearsal for murder and a statement on man. "Don't look," the father tells the boy. But Dostoevsky forces the reader to look at the beating, at the crowd, at himself. ("Man on the surface of the earth does not have the right to turn away.") "My property!" screams the peasant Mikolka in his drunken rage on three separate occasions, as he violently smashes away at the mare. This is a scene of absolute evil: here surface in a strange symbiosis what for Dostoevsky are the most predatory instincts in man: violence, sensuality and property-mindedness. The message of "my property" (*moyo dobro*) is clear: what is mine, what I covet and own, releases me from all moral obligations, because it is *my* good that is involved; the use of the word "*dobro*" here—property, goods, but also ethical "good"—subtly suggests the smashing of all moral norms or "barriers," the triumph of raw egoism over any moral imperative in human relations. "My property! What I want—I go ahead and do!" (*Chto*

---

[8] The contrasts here reflect, of course, the fundamental creative tension Dostoevsky posits in human existence between man's quest for the moral and aesthetic ideal, on the one hand, and his earthly nature with its potential for violence and deformation, on the other. See my discussion of this problem in *Dostoevsky's Quest for Form: A Study of His Philosophy of Art* (New Haven: Yale University Press, 1966), in particular pp. 40–70.

khochu, to i delaju!) "Now I shall do just as I want with all of you because I have lost control of myself," cries the murderer of Akulka in *Notes from the House of the Dead*. The motif "all is permissible" permeates Raskolnikov's nightmare, as it does "Akulka's Husband" and Ivan's stories of the cruelties inflicted on children. This is a grim statement on man.

Others, too, participate in the orgy of violence, or watch passively from the sidelines, laugh, enjoy the spectacle, or just go on "cracking nuts." There are some voices of condemnation. But they are drowned out. Even the old man who shouts indignantly—"What are you about, are you a Christian or a devil?"—becomes demonized, is unable, finally, to restrain his laughter as he watches the mare, "a bag of bones," kicking about.

"Thank God, this is only a dream!" exclaims Raskolnikov. But the dream was out of Russian life; reality, Dostoevsky liked to emphasize, was more fantastic than fiction. The mare-beating scene is the center of world evil, and it is not surprising that at this moment, on the threshold of crime, Raskolnikov's soul was "in confusion and darkness."

Are the people who inhabit Raskolnikov's nightmare "monsters" or "victims"? Ivan's question—and it is really Raskolnikov's as well—is very much to the point here: "the real issue is whether all this comes from people's bad qualities or simply because it is their nature." Raskolnikov's nightmare—the terrible event at its center—provides a tragic answer to this question; and if human nature is a moral wasteland, then "there are no barriers, and that is as it should be!" Raskolnikov's social-philosophical *conclusions*—here embodied in the action of his own psychodrama—represent a precipitous movement toward murder.

Certainly, the fractured character of Raskolnikov's moral consciousness is revealed in this dream. The boy identifies with the suffering mare, with the victim, as Raskolnikov does, initially, in his various encounters in Part One. Here there is anguish to the point of hysteria. The boy cries and screams and at the end puts his arm around the mare's "dead, bloodstained muzzle, and kissed her, kissed her on the eyes, on the mouth." But, as in Raskolnikov's waking hours, anguish turns into rage, and the boy "suddenly leaps up and flings himself on Mikolka, striking out in a frenzy with his fists." Mikolka is clearly the oppressor, the embodiment of the principle of self-will. He may easily stand in for types like the pawnbroker, Luzhin, or Svidrigailov, vicious people exploiting and degrading innocent people like Dunia, Lizaveta, or Sonia, quiet timid creatures with gentle eyes like those of the mare. It is against these vicious people that Raskolnikov revolts. But in his revolt he is himself transformed into a monstrous, shapeless Mikolka, and himself becomes the alien oppressor, exalted by a new morality that crushes the "guilty" and innocent alike. In the image of the child, then, Raskolnikov recoils from the horror that Raskolnikov, the man, contemplates; but in the image of Mikolka, Raskolnikov prefigures his own role as murderer. Raskolnikov's dream has often been described as revealing the last efforts of his moral conscience to resist the crime. This is true: the dream is a battle; but it is a battle that is *lost*. On the philosophical plane, as a statement on man, the dream is the tragic finale to the pro and contra of Part One, the final smashing of "barriers."

The dream gives expression, finally, to a central paradox. Here is hell, or, in any case, the postfall world plunged in terrible evil. Yet the evil is witnessed and judged essentially from the point of view of the innocent, prefall mentality of the child. The world of the "fathers"—the adaptors, objectively indifferent to good and evil—is discredited ("Come along and don't look . . . it's not our business"); their Christianity at best (witness the "old man") is shameful and frightening: Christian ethics dissolve into the aesthetics of laughter, the enjoyment of suffering, a Sadean realm that Dostoevsky explored in *Notes from the House of the Dead*. The Christian ethos is not in men's hearts. The church is out of town, literally, but also in a metaphorical sense: it is *hors de combat*, passive. The real, active tension in the nightmare—dramatic and ideological—is in the almost Quixote-like opposition of absolute evil with absolute innocence: the inflamed demonic violence and sensuality of Mikolka, and the pure, idyllic sensibility, goodness, and anguish of the child. But the child, though rightfully protesting cruelty and evil, is unable conceptually to integrate evil in his prefall universe. This is essentially the problem, as Dostoevsky conceives it, of such types as Raskolnikov and Ivan: idealists, humanists, they are unable, at root, to disencumber themselves of their utopian dreams, their insistence on the moral absolute. Raskolnikov, very much like his sister, is a chaste soul.

In the final analysis, what Dostoevsky finds missing in Raskolnikov (and, perhaps, in himself as well) is precisely a calm, reconciling Christian perspective, precisely an attitude that, while never yielding to evil, nonetheless, in ultimate terms, accepts it as part of God's universe, as cloaked in the mystery of God's truth. Such a perspective, indeed, we find in Zosima in *The Brothers Karamazov*. Dostoevsky strained in this direction, made his final conscious choice in this direction, indeed gives clear evidence of this choice (Raskolnikov's ultimate choice, we must believe) in the prelude to the nightmare. Yet at the same time he invested the child's suffering and rage with deep pathos and anguish. The child's pure nature is ill-equipped to cope with reality or even grasp the deeper coherence of life's processes. Yet it seems a cardinal feature of Dostoevsky's own outlook that all genuine moral feeling must arise from an open confrontation of the pure ideal with reality. Such a confrontation, on the plane of everyday life, may be unpleasant, disruptive, unrealistic, even absurd; but as Ivan Karamazov observes to Alyosha, "absurdities are frightfully necessary on earth. The world rests on absurdities, and without them, perhaps, nothing would ever have taken place in it." In Raskolnikov's nightmare only the pure vision of the child, only the sacred indignation of an unsullied soul, holds out any hope to a world that is all but damned.

"Freedom! freedom!" is Raskolnikov's predominant sensation after his nightmare. "He was free now from that witchcraft, that sorcery, those spells, that obsession." (I, 5) The nightmare is catharsis, purgation, momentary relief; it is only a "dream"; yet this "dream" brings him face-to-face with himself. "God! . . . will I really? Will I really take the ax, will I really hit her on the head, split open her skull, will I really slip in the sticky warm blood," he reflects on awakening. "Good Lord, will I really?" The day before, he recalls, he had recoiled from the idea of crime in sick horror. And now he remarks inwardly, and significantly: "Granted . . . that everything [his plans for the murder] . . . is clear as arithmetic" but "really I know that I shall never decide on it in spite of everything!" Indeed, Raskolnikov will never *decide* to commit the crime, never consciously, actively and with his whole moral being, choose to kill or—the reverse—choose *not* to kill. His "moral resolution of the question" will never go deeper than "casuistry." (I, 6) And yet he will kill! He will lose his "freedom" (which in any case, after his nightmare, is deceptive) and be *pulled* into crime and murder (so it will seem to him) by some "unnatural power." Like Ivan Karamazov—but unlike Ivan's brother Dmitry—Raskolnikov will *allow* circumstances to shape his destiny. Here a contrast with Dmitry is instructive. Dmitry spent the two days before the murder of his father (which he did not, in the end, commit) "literally casting himself in all directions, 'struggling with his fate and saving himself,' as he himself put it later." Dmitry's open, if naive, recognition of his opposite impulses and freedom to kill or not to kill, as well as his awareness of competing "philosophies" within him, are the crucial internal factors that help to "save" him in the end from the crime of murder. Raskolnikov's dialectic of consciousness also constitutes a struggle, but his dialectic moves him toward, not away, from the crime; in the end, one "philosophy" triumphs: he loses his freedom (he blames the crime, significantly, on the "devil") and yields to his obsession; Dmitry, on the other hand, triumphs over his obsession (and, equally significantly, attributes his victory to "God").

Raskolnikov's deeply passive relationship to his crime often has been noted.[9] Yet this passivity is not a purely psychological phenomenon; it is, Dostoevsky clearly indicates, closely linked with Raskolnikov's world outlook, an area of very intense *activity* for Raskolnikov. As Raskolnikov realizes later on—and as his own thinking and language suggest—he is dominated at the time of the crime by a belief in "fate," a general superstitious concern for all sorts of chthonic forces, perhaps even a taste for the occult (elements that, in Svidrigailov, have already surfaced in the

[9] See, for example, W. D. Snodgrass, "*Crime and Punishment*: The Tenor of Part One," *The Hudson Review*, 13 (1960): 241.

form of "ghosts"). Raskolnikov's problem is directly alluded to in Dostoevsky's notes to the novel. "That was an evil spirit: How otherwise could I have overcome all those difficulties?" Raskolnikov observes at one point. And a few lines later these significant lines: "I should have done that. (*There is no free will. Fatalism*)." And, finally, these crucial thoughts: "Now why has my life ended? Grumble: But God does not exist and so forth." Dostoevsky's own thought emerges even in these few notes: a loss of faith in God—or in the meaningfulness of God's universe—must end with the individual abandoning himself to a notion of "fate."

Raskolnikov shares his proclivity toward fatalism with a number of Dostoevsky's heroes, for example, the man from the "underground," the hero of "A Gentle Creature," and Aleksey Petrovich (*The Gambler,* 1866).[10] The similarity between Raskolnikov's and the gambler's problems is striking. Both are dominated by a sterile, rationalistic outlook; both place themselves in a position of challenging "fate"; both lose their moral awareness in the essential act of challenge (murder, gambling); both seek through their acts to attain to an absolute freedom from the so-called laws of nature that are binding on ordinary men; both, in the end, conceive of themselves as victims of "fate." Such types continually are seeking their cues or directives outside of themselves. Quite symptomatic, in this connection, is Raskolnikov's prayerful remark after his dream: "O God! show me the way, that I may renounce this cursed dream of mine!"

The fateful "circumstance" that struck Raskolnikov "almost to the point of superstition" and that seemed a "predestination of his fate" (I, 5) was his chance meeting with Lizaveta, a meeting that, in Raskolnikov's view, sets into motion the machinery of fate. Raskolnikov returned home after that meeting "like a man condemned to death. He had not reasoned anything out, he was quite incapable of reasoning; but suddenly with all his being he felt that his mind and will were no longer free, and that everything had suddenly been finally decided." (I, 5) Similarly, Raskolnikov responds to the conversation he overhears in a restaurant—by "coincidence" two men give expression to "precisely the same thoughts" that had been cropping up in his own mind—as "something preordained, some guiding hint":

> This last day . . . which had so unexpectedly decided everything at once, had caught him up almost automatically, as if by the hand, and pulled him along with unnatural power, blindly, irresistibly, and with no objections on his part; and he was caught, as if by the hem of his coat in the cog of a wheel, and being drawn in. (I, 6)

[10] *The Gambler,* of course, was written at the time Dostoevsky was finishing *Crime and Punishment,* and it reflects Dostoevsky's preoccupation with Raskolnikov's state of mind. For a perceptive study of *The Gambler,* see D. S. Savage, "The Idea of *The Gambler,*" *Sewanee Review,* 58 (April, 1950): 281–98. For a consideration of the problem of chance and fate in "A Gentle Creature," see my essay "On the Uses of the Motif of the Duel in Dostoevsky's 'A Gentle Creature,'" in *Canadian-American Slavic Studies,* 6, no. 2 (Summer, 1972): 256–64.

Dostoevsky is not projecting an "accident" theory of personal history; but neither does he deny the role of chance. Chance is the eternal "given"; without it there would be no freedom. Raskolnikov's encounter with Lizaveta was accidental (though not pure accident); it was by chance that he overheard the conversation in which he recognized his own thoughts (although, as Dostoevsky wrote in his letter to M. N. Katkov on the novel, the ideas that infect Raskolnikov "are floating about in the air"). But these chance elements only set into motion a course of action that was seeking to be born, albeit without the full sanction of moral self.

What is crucial in Raskolnikov's situation is not so much the factor of chance as *his disposition to be guided by chance*, his readiness, as it were, to gamble, to seek out and acknowledge in chance his so-called "fate." [11] What is crucial to his action is the general state of consciousness that he brings to the moment of critical accident: and consciousness here is not only his nervous, overwrought state, but the way he conceives of his relationship to the world. Such is the background of Tolstoy's perception that Raskolnikov's true moment of decision and his "true life" occurred not when he met the sister of the old lady, not at the time of the murder when he was "mechanically" discharging the energy accumulated in him, "not when he was acting, but when he was thinking, when his consciousness alone was working"—and in realms affecting the total scope of his existence.

Raskolnikov seized upon the various chance incidents that preceded the murder as the action of "fate," but did not recognize that fate here had all the iron logic of his own, inner fatality. His passivity—that state of drift in which he evades the necessity of choice and abandons all moral responsibility—is motivated, then, not only by his deep and unresolved moral conflicts but by a muddled rationalistic, *fatalistic* outlook that itself denies freedom of choice or moral responsibility, an outlook that in the end posits an incoherent universe. This outlook is not something that Raskolnikov merely picked up in reading or table talk. The sense of a blind, meaningless universe, of a loveless world dominated by an "evil spirit" [12]—and this is conveyed by Part One—emerges from Raskolnikov's confrontation with the concrete social reality of Russian life, with the tragedy of the "lower depths": its hopeless poverty, its degradation, its desolation. It is this confrontation with the human condition that violates the purity of Raskolnikov's ideal, that ruptures his faith in moral law and human nature, that bends him toward a tragic view of man and

[11] The same conception is at the basis of Tolstoy's psychologically profound presentation of Anna Karenina's first meeting with Vronsky at the railroad station. See my essay, "Chance and Design in *Anna Karenina*," in *The Disciplines of Criticism*, edited by Peter Demetz et al. (New Haven: Yale University Press, 1968), pp. 315–329.

[12] The idea of an "evil spirit" as the embodiment of oppressive fate crops up in *Winter Notes on Summer Impressions* (1863) where Dostoevsky speaks in the chapter "Baal" of a "proud spirit" dominating all the misery and squalor of London.

toward a universe ruled by "blind fate." [13] It is this confrontation—in which compassion and contempt for man form an intimate dialectic—that nourishes the related structures of his "ideas" or ideology: his altruistic utilitarian ethics and his Napoleonic self-exaltation and contempt for the "herd." It is this confrontation that underlies his murder of the old pawnbroker.

Consciousness, of course, is not passive here. Raskolnikov, half-deranged in the isolation and darkness of his incomprehensible universe (the model of which is his little coffinlike room), actively reaches out into "history," into his loveless universe to rationalize his own responses to reality and his own psychological needs. He is an intellectual. His "ideas," moreover, acquire a dynamic of their own, raise him to new levels of abstraction and fantasy, and provide him, finally, with a "theoretical" framework and justification for crime. Yet, whatever the independence of these "ideas" (as we find them in his article or circulating freely in taverns and restaurants), they acquire their vitality, their force only insofar as they mediate the confrontation between individual consciousness and social reality; only insofar as they give expression to Raskolnikov's intimate social and psychological experience, to his deepest, organic responses to the world about him.

In one of his notebooks, Dostoevsky refers to himself with pride as the first to focus on

> the tragedy of the underground: it consists of suffering, self-punishment, the consciousness of something better and the impossibility of achieving that "something"; and, chiefly, it consists in the clear conviction of these unhappy people that all are alike and hence it is not even worth trying to improve. Consolation? Faith? There is consolation from no one, faith in no one. But another step from here and one finds depravity, crime (murder). Mystery.

The profoundly responsive Raskolnikov, one might say, voluntarily takes on himself that "tragedy of the underground," experiences it internally, morally, in all its aspects and agonizing contradictions. His final "step" should have been love—a step *toward* humanity; instead, experiencing the tragedy of life too deeply, and drawing from that tragedy the most extreme social and philosophical conclusions, Raskolnikov (a victim of his own solitude, ratiocination, and casuistry), took a step *away* from humanity into crime, murder, mystery.

Such is the practical denouement of the philosophical pro and contra —the dialectic of consciousness of Raskolnikov—in Part One.

---

[13] See, in this connection, Raskolnikov's bitter complaint about "blind fate," in the epilogue (chap. 2).

Raskolnikov

by Jacques Madaule

Art may consist in introducing an artificial order where, in reality, disorder reigns; this is the way of many writers who are highly praised by their contemporaries. Dostoevsky was not one of these writers. He aspired to an authentic order. While the purpose of art is not to create order, it can at least suggest it. Of course, all art in a certain sense involves order, choice and structuring—and this is true also of the art of Dostoevsky, in spite of the way it may sometimes seem. We may view the five great novels of the second part of his career as a dialectical development. Their particular focus is the study of the ravages committed by Western rationalism on the Russian spirit, the disorder it has introduced, and the means at the disposal of the Russian spirit not so much rudely to repulse this rationalism as to assimilate what is legitimate and inevitable in it, so as to create a new order. Here, at least, is the most obvious problem. We shall see, later, that there are others more profound and more crucial.

It is appropriate to note the particular importance in this connection of *Notes from the Underground,* a short work written in 1864. Part One is given over to a kind of confession of a minor Petersburg civil servant. Nowhere, perhaps, better than here can we grasp the naked reality of evil. If rationalism is incapable of ever organizing the human world, it is because evil is in man as an unalterable quantity. The civil servant imagines a situation in which mankind would be subjected to a scientific prescription for happiness. This possibility would not seem to exceed the capacity of human reason. But then what happens?

> I would not be at all surprised, for instance, if suddenly and without the slightest possible reason a gentleman of an ignoble or rather a reactionary and sardonic countenance were to arise amid all that future reign of universal common sense and, gripping his sides firmly with his hands, were to say to us all, "Well, gentlemen, what about giving all this common sense a mighty kick and letting it scatter in the dust before our feet simply to send

"Raskolnikov," chapter 3 from Le Christianisme de Dostoïevsky, *by Jacques Madaule. Copyright 1938 by Librairie Bloud & Gay (Paris). Translated from the French by Robert Louis Jackson. Reprinted by permission of the author and publisher.*

all these logarithms to the devil so that we can again live according to our foolish will?" That wouldn't matter, either, but for the regrettable fact that he would certainly find followers: for man is made like that. (I, 7) [1]

In other words, over and above his reason is his will. No doubt we are not free to resist that which is rationally manifest. But it is our reason alone which is not free. When it is fettered, our will remains independent. We can will something else, even that two plus two equals five. That sum may please us precisely because it is absurd. One will say, perhaps, that this is evil. And, indeed, all evil, it would seem, comes from this assent to the absurd; from our susceptibility to giving preference to suffering—our own and, of course, that of others as well—over what seems on the surface our true interest.

But is evil the only result? Rationalism is beyond good and evil. Only with freedom does one begin to discern good and evil, and freedom is not in reason but in will. Rationalism denies human freedom. The revolt against the scientific order, the rejection of a happiness which we do not share is not only the effect of our malice; it is also the irreducible claim of our freedom. All of man's grandeur lies in this freedom. His secret temptation is to free himself of it and get rid of the burden of it—a rationalist temptation which had a strong grip on the Russian spirit in the middle of the last century.

If we wish to find out what the Russian people are really like, at least as Dostoevsky saw them, we must turn to *Notes from the House of the Dead.* The Russian people, even in their most profound degradation, are Christ-bearers. The upper classes of society have turned away from Christ as well as from the people. They have been seduced by the West. They have assimilated Western sciences very rapidly—too rapidly indeed—and these sciences have corrupted even their language. In an amusing page from his *Diary of a Writer,* Dostoevsky shows us those Russians who, when abroad, pretend to speak only French and who succeed only in speaking French as badly as their own language. Communication is no longer possible with the great mass of people who continue to live as their ancestors did. Thus, the intelligentsia is, as it were, superimposed on the Russian people. This separation, however, is not so great as to deprive these educated intellectuals of a specifically Russian quality—hence their anguish, their dissatisfaction, their disequilibrium. They have taken literally, with a profound naiveté concealed by a surface cynicism, the affirmations of Western reason. From the moment that they no longer believe in God, and while they are looking forward to a rational organization of the world to come, "all is permissible." For their part the humble people look up in wonder at this misleading example. Although rationalism does not touch them deeply, they too know that "all is permissible"—

---

[1] From *The Best Short Stories of Dostoevsky.* Translated with an Introduction by David T. Magarshack (New York: Modern Library, Inc., n.d.) [ED.]

as, for example, Smerdyakov in *The Brothers Karamazov*. But let us not look ahead.

The people bear in themselves almost infinite resources of patience, resignation, love. Dostoevsky experienced them when in Siberia he lived cheek-by-jowl with the convicts. He was reborn among these simple beings, by and large more unfortunate than guilty. It was in prison that he definitively discarded the doctrines that had led him to prison. He does not sufficiently distinguish his faith in the people from his faith in Christ. This populism, which was more or less the error of all the Slavophiles (although Dostoevsky never integrally shared their doctrines) is perhaps the great sin of noble and generous souls in the last century. Under the pretext of rendering to the people the honor that was incontestably its due, they exaggerated its merits. To be in touch with the truth, it is not enough to be of the people, and Dostoevsky would not have been so grossly deceived about the Orthodox Christ, which he opposes to the Catholic Christ of Rome, if he had not been led into error by his faith in the Russian people.

Be that as it may, from this double point of departure *Crime and Punisment* becomes possible. Rodion Romanovich Raskolnikov is typical of those intellectuals who have been led astray, who have not lost all their conscience nor all their generosity, but who think that the old morality is out of date and that a superior man is not always obliged to obey the injunctions to the letter. He gives himself over to an experiment. The murder of an old usurer who appears to have done nothing but evil in her life, who is not useful to anybody and hateful to everybody: do we not have here an obstacle that we have the right to overturn? Is not murder an act that we have the right to dare? It will be noted that however poor he is it is not his poverty that drives him to crime. He had many other ways of getting along, such as throwing himself wholeheartedly into work or having recourse to the generosity of his friend Razumikhin. But the murder is a "model" act—one of those acts which one must commit to be sure of escaping the limits of ordinary humanity. In Raskolnikov's situation Napoleon would not have hesitated, he thinks.

· One must be fairly sturdy to carry out such a heinous crime. Raskolnikov puts himself to the test. Not only his own future, but perhaps that of all humanity depends on its results. With evil one can do good. We have rejected the vulgar notions of good and evil, anyway. There is no such thing as evil in itself, just as there is no absolute good. The morality of the strong cannot be that of the weak. Now just here the crime overwhelms Raskolnikov, and that is the whole tragedy: because other than rational values are involved in crime. We are not masters of life. Vainly do we calculate everything down to the last detail: along comes the unexpected to confound us. He had to kill not only the old pawnbroker, but Lizaveta as well, a simple and innocent creature. Raskolnikov no longer had a choice.

And now comes the punishment. It is not penal servitude, of which we barely get a glimpse and where the criminal will find in suffering the source of his own resurrection. Neither is it remorse, in the sense that one ordinarily gives to this term. Rather, it seems to me, it is the sudden collapse of a whole mental universe. Raskolnikov find himself in that immense crowd of the insulted and injured who never cease to be present for Dostoevsky. They are the limbs of the suffering Christ; the unbearable reproach abides in them. In his dream of glory the young student had forgotten them. They flow back towards him, as soon as the crime is committed, and envelop him in their destiny. Here is the one who has prostituted herself to come to the aid of her undeserving parents (undeserving? truly more unfortunate than undeserving). But Sonia has not lost her purity. I know very well all the jokes that one makes about these courtesans of pure heart of whom romanticism has somewhat taken advantage. There is no doubt that Dostoevsky had a dose of sentimentalism "à la Schiller" which he was later to criticize so often. Nonetheless, if ever a character in a drama was necessary, that one is Sonia, and Sonia just as we find her, that is to say, a "chaste and wilted" Sonia.

In the abyss into which he sank of his own will, Raskolnikov can be reached only by somedoy who partakes to some degree of his own degradation; and it is Sonia who suspects the crime and who forces the confession. There is also, of course, Porfiry Petrovich, the examining magistrate, who shares the Western culture of Raskolnikov, and who plays with him as a cat with a mouse. But Porfiry Petrovich would not have sufficed. Raskolnikov would still have been able victoriously to escape his rigorous deductions had it not been for the mortal weakness into which he is plunged by his contact with Sonia. It is here that we take the measure of the whole depth of Dostoevsky's "realism." No sooner does one wish to penetrate to the depth of truth of things than one perceives that they exist on several planes. There is the juridical and rational plane where Porfiry Petrovich operates. He investigates the motives of the crime; he understands the mechanics of it and, at times, he enjoys it as an enlightened connoisseur. But nothing in him is capable of forcing the confession which is indispensable in the absence of material evidence. This confession must be spontaneous, must come from the depths of freedom, that is to say, in the final analysis, from the place out of which the crime itself emerged.

Here is where Sonia comes in: she is completely incapable of analyzing the motives for the act, but she senses the fault because she is aware of the unhappiness. For her Raskolnikov is nothing else than a being infinitely more miserable than she is herself. She does not condemn him, because we do not have the right to judge our fellow man. She pities him. She wants to share his cross, to take part of a burden so heavy that he who is carrying it succumbs under the load. Thus, Raskolnikov is introduced into another world—one which neither the devotion of his mother nor the purity of his sister nor the generous dedication of Razumikhin led him to suspect: a world where each person suffers for everybody, and where everybody suffers for each, in Christ.

So ends that life in which the superior man, be it at the price of what vulgar morality calls a crime, doles out happiness to humanity. Raskolnikov, reduced here to the level of the most humble and despised, is forced to accept his own salvation from Sonia, and to receive in exchange a suffering that he has not chosen. This defeat of a man which can only change into victory through a confession of weakness appears before us in infinitely more atrocious form in the person of Svidrigailov. He is one of those astounding characters in Dostoevsky who are human only in appearance. He was preceded in *The Insulted and Injured* by Prince Valkovsky with his terrifying confession to the narrator. Here is an excerpt in which this infamous man explains his case by an anecdote:

> There was a crazy official in Paris, who was afterwards put into a madhouse when it was realized that he was mad. Well, when he went out of his mind this is what he thought of to amuse himself. He undressed at home, altogether, like Adam, only keeping on his shoes and socks, put on an ample cloak that came down to his heels, wrapped himself round in it, and with a grave and majestic air went out into the street. Well, if he's looked at sideways—he's a man like anyone else, going for a walk in a long cloak to please himself. But whenever he met anyone in a lonely place where there was no one else about, he walked up to him in silence, and with the most serious and profoundly thoughtful air suddenly stopped before him, threw open his cloak and displayed himself in all the . . . purity of his heart! That used to last for a minute, then he would wrap himself up again, and in silence, without moving a muscle of his face, he would stalk by the petrified spectator, as grave and majestic as the ghost in Hamlet. That was how he used to behave with every one, men, women, and children, and that was his only pleasure. Well, some degree of the same pleasure may be experienced when one flabbergasts some romantic Schiller, by putting out one's tongue at him when he least expects it. (III, 10) [2]

This cynicism, it is clear, has almost nothing in common with the relatively pleasant barrel where Diogenes lodged. In fact, it is not cynicism; it is despair. And that must end logically with the suicide of Svidrigailov as with that of Smerdyakov.

Svidrigailov is situated, in *Crime and Punishment,* at the edge of the drama. He plays there, without doubt, an important "supporting" role, but this role could have been taken by somebody else; moreover, it was not necessary to stress this character so strongly had Dostoevsky not had another purpose beyond telling the story of Raskolnikov. But because, since 1860, he had returned again and again to one and the same subject, he was always tempted to view it each time from a different aspect. Ras-

[2] From *The Insulted and Injured*, in *The Novels of Fyodor Dostoevsky* 6, trans. Constance Garnett (New York: The Macmillan Co., n.d.).

kolnikov marks a moment of the fall; a moment where, whatever be the crime, the possibility of a redemptive punishment still remains. With Svidrigailov we touch the bottom of the abyss, we penetrate into a kind of earthly hell. There is nothing, moreover, that the damned does not know of his condition. From that obscure moment when he agreed to the supreme abjuration, all exits are closed to him and his eyes are opened.

> "What if there are only spiders there—or something of that sort?" "That's insane," thought Raskolnikov. "We always imagine eternity as a conception impossible to grasp, something enormous, immense! Why must it inevitably be enormous? Just think of a single little room—a bathhouse in one of our backwater villages, something like that, sooty spiders in all the corners—and that's all there is to eternity. You know, sometimes that's the way it strikes me." "You mean, you mean to tell me," said Raskolnikov with a queasy feeling, "you mean you can't imagine anything more comforting than that, more just?" Svidrigailov replied, smiling vaguely: "More just? How do we know? Maybe it is just. I'll tell you something. If I had my way, that's exactly the way I would have made it!" (IV, 1)

Here, to be sure, is a mystery of mysteries and the causes of Svidrigailov's damnation remain obscure. Nevertheless, we know his history well enough to understand that he has deliberately chosen evil. Although these sinister gentlemen affect reasonableness with a polish of Western ideas (though they seldom read) and their maxim is, since all is permissible, that everybody must follow exclusively his own instinct, it turns out that this instinct is not neutral. We may let ourselves be deceived a moment by appearances and see in them only ordinary *bons vivants* with few scruples. But when we look at them more closely their true nature is not slow to reveal itself. He who does not choose good, necessarily chooses evil. Now what is evil if not suffering inflicted gratuitously, and as though out of pleasure, on an innocent creature?

Such is absolute evil. Although he had committed a double murder, and one of his victims, at least, was precisely such an innocent creature, yet Raskolnikov has not committed the absolute evil. The notion of the distinction between good and evil remains alive in him even when he contemplated his crime. He believed in a double morality: a broad one for superior beings and a narrow one for the generality of men. He did not entertain a blanket notion of "all is permissible." He had pitied the Marmeladov family, and it is this pity which saved him, which earned him the help of Sonia. But Svidrigailov preferred evil, this absolute evil, which is suffering inflicted for nothing on an innocent creature. In order to understand what is happening, then, one must analyze Russian boredom, such, in any case, as it appeared to Dostoevsky.

This boredom, for absentee landlords and the poorly educated like Svidrigailov or Fyodor Karamazov, may be explained by purely natural and, to some extent, sociological motives:

"How could I not? There was a whole crowd of us about eight years ago, all highly respectable. We used to pass the time. We were people with manners, mind you. Some were poets, some capitalists. Have you noticed, by the way, that in our Russian society generally you'll find the very best manners among those who have been kicked around? Just now I've let myself go a bit, living in the country, and all that." (IV, 1)

All the same, it is clear that this explanation is inadequate. The life of absentee landlords in Russia in the middle of the last century did not appreciably differ, if we take into account other evidence, from that of their opposite numbers in the same period in other parts of Europe. The boredom from which they suffer in Dostoevsky is a veritable sickness of the soul. Fundamentally, we are dealing with the same boredom of which Baudelaire speaks in his prefatory poem, "Au lecteur" in *Les Fleurs du Mal*.

This boredom is man's affirmation of his own solitude, that irremediable solitude in which man finds himself when he sets his face against God and thereby against communion with other men; it is a metaphysical boredom. There is little doubt that Dostoevsky was himself the victim of that kind of boredom. He was born at a time when the spirit realized that nothing matters—not even, indeed, the satisfaction of those instincts which seem innate to it. One yawns, and does any old thing; but what one does then is always evil. A sick soul continually calls for a stronger and stronger wine. This wine can only be that of suffering. There is no error more naive than to believe that man seeks happiness. He convinces himself that he does; but, in reality, happiness which results from the permanent absence of real suffering (for the happiness at issue here is a purely negative one) is boring. The soul no longer seems to live, and this state resembles death—but one in which time would continue to flow with an inexpressible slowness; a death whose victim would be continually witnessing his own nothingness. How, then, does one feel oneself alive if not by making others suffer for it? And there is no suffering more exquisite for man than that which he brings about through his own cruelty. For man, if he is not naturally good, is capable of feeling pity. We know that Schopenhauer wanted to found morality on this natural pity. No heart can fail to be secretly touched by the impotent moans of the oppressed. This state is a suffering which is accompanied by a pleasure and pity for ourselves. The road which leads from a somewhat facile sentimentality to a more perverse cruelty is a road quickly traversed. Do we not hear of Alexander of Phères, one of the cruelest tyrants recorded by Antiquity, that he could not witness without tears the misfortunes of the heroes of tragedies? There is a still more certain means of making these tears flow: it is to become the agent of the suffering which justifies them. In these depths suffering and pleasure unite in the same spasm.

Do not think, moreover, that the perverse man exercises this cruelty solely on others. He exercises it first with a voluptuous refinement on himself. Svidrigailov began by degrading himself in his country solitude, and he drew from this degradation as much sorrow as pleasure. The cynicism of a Prince Valkovsky is only apparently serene. It pains him to reveal his loathsome nudity before the narrator. Dissatisfied with himself, incapable through his own weakness of the effort which would be necessary to control himself, he has long abandoned himself, like an exhausted dog flowing with the current. But he suffers from it, and that is why he exhibits his own humiliation, so as to redouble his suffering and draw from it a more exquisite delight. This strange face which looks at him with horror is not that of an unknown person whom he has drawn into a cabaret by chance: it is his own. He watches himself suffer, for he too has been a "Schiller" in his youth. And it is the same when Svidrigailov faces Raskolnikov.

These degraded beings, after all, however stupid they be in other respects (and Dostoevsky often indulgently stresses their great stupidity), are always endowed with a formidable lucidity. They choose with perfect aim their witnesses or their victims. Raskolnikov, laden with his crime, in some kind of automatic way, creates around him complementary characters. Svidrigailov is no less necessary than Sonia, when one looks at the drama on this level. They are both drawn by the same smell of murder, the one an angel of light, and the other an angel of darkness. They take their positions around the criminal in order to mark his place exactly. A soul to save and a soul to lose. Or rather, they are the salvation and the damnation which are simultaneously offered to Raskolnikov, so that he might make the decisive choice in full knowledge of the case. Svidrigailov has no more need than Sonia herself to hear the confession of the crime in order to know who Raskolnikov is. It is striking that these are the two privileged witnesses to that confession. Nothing better demonstrates the true theatre of the Dostoevsky novel which opens on the abyss above and the abyss below, that of the heavens and that of hell.

A Great Philosophical Novel

by Nicholas M. Chirkov

Crime and Punishment is one of Dostoevsky's outstanding philosophical novels. Its ideas have been the subject of endless critical interpretation. In addition, it is, for the 1860s, a highly relevant and topical novel, depicting graphically the social life of Russia after the 1861 reforms[1] and raising Dostoevsky's social novel to a height never before attained. On another score, *Crime and Punishment* is a polemical novel, full of the public issues of the day. And Dostoevsky, militant publicist of his epoch, makes his presence felt every step of the way.

Crime and Punishment is first of all a novel about Russian capitalism, its manifestations and effects at the beginning of the post-reform period. But in what form or shape does capitalism present itself to the reader? An atmosphere of general trafficking and exploitation is immediately noticeable in those first forays of Raskolnikov onto the streets of the city. We do not see capitalist production in its organizing role at that stage of capitalism. There is nothing to indicate the progressive significance of capitalism for the historical moment which Dostoevsky describes. Capitalism in *Crime and Punishment* is shown exclusively in its destructive aspects.

Two characters are particularly important for an understanding of the essence of capitalism in this novel: the old pawnbroker, Aliona Ivanovna, and Peter Petrovich Luzhin, Dunia Raskolnikov's fiancé. Both figures are portrayed in their extreme deformity. The moral deformity of the wizened old lady, the "louse," is reflected in her outer appearance. In our first view of Luzhin, in Raskolnikov's "ship's cabin," Dostoevsky accents the decorous, proper bridegroom, his strikingly modish dress, his sleek, manufactured appearance. His propriety, however, conceals an

From the chapter "Velikij filosofskij roman" ["A Great Philosophical Novel"] in O stile Dostoevskogo [Dostoevsky's Style] by N. M. Chirkov (Moscow, 1967), pp. 78–114. Translated by Cerylle A. Fritts. Chirkov worked on his book on Dostoevsky (from which this essay is abstracted) for a period of twenty years; he submitted it as a doctoral dissertation in the late 1940s. But in the conditions of the Stalinist period he was afforded no opportunity to defend his dissertation. Part of his work on Dostoevsky was published posthumously in 1963. [ED.]

[1] Russian serfdom was abolished by imperial rescript in 1861 and a number of social and economic reforms were instituted. [ED.]

experienced "wheeler-dealer," a swindler capable of every kind of vileness (see, for example, the scene at Marmeladov's funeral gathering).

Dostoevsky uses Luzhin as the spokesman for the "philosophy of the age"—the philosophy of the "whole coat," of extreme utilitarianism and of the complete justification of the existing social order. One notes Luzhin's smug social optimism. He advocates a consistent philosophy of naked egoism which, in his opinion, is the guarantee of the prosperity and well-being of all society. "Now science says: Love yourself above all, for everything in the world is based on self-interest. If you love yourself above all, you will manage your business properly, and your coat will remain whole. Economic science adds that the more successfully private business is run in society and the more (so to speak) whole coats there are, the firmer are its foundations and the more the commonweal flourishes." (II, 5) Luzhin's program is the familiar program of so-called "economic freedom"; in other words, it is an outright apology for the principle of capitalist competition.

The figures of the old pawnbroker and Luzhin are not only significant for Dostoevsky in themselves. More important is how Dostoevsky as author relates to these characters—the emotional tone of his artistic presentation. This tone is one of constant aversion and, with respect to Luzhin, of outright sarcasm. Dostoevsky does not simply describe his characters, but constantly polemicizes with them.

The capitalist ethos is further expressed in the atmosphere of acquisitiveness, speculation and profiteering which encompasses even the minor townfolk in *Crime and Punishment*. The novel is thronged with a multitude of rapacious petty traffickers: street hawkers, proprietors of taverns and "establishments," where liquor is consumed on the premises and sold "to take out," and peddlars in the Haymarket with rags, rubbish, and all kinds of junk. Hopeless and utter poverty exists inseparably from this petty thievery and profiteering. Rag-pickers and "industrialists" appear side by side throughout the novel. Raskolnikov himself at the beginning of the novel is described as a "ragamuffin and a rag-picker." Inseparable from poverty, finally, is prostitution.

Crime and Punishment picks up and carries on the motif of prostitution, which had been introduced earlier in *Notes from the Underground*. In his development of this motif Doestoevsky employs the stylistic devices of emotional and thematic repetition or echo. At every stage of the novel, Raskolnikov experiences certain recurring impressions: especially striking are those created by Marmeladov's story of Sonia's plight and by the letter Raskolnikov receives from his mother, which describes Dunia's predicament, its possible outcome. Raskolnikov cannot fail to link the fates of Sonia and Dunia: "O loving and unjust hearts! Indeed! We would even go the same way as Sonia! Dear little Sonia, Sonia Marmeladova, Sonia eternal, as long as the world endures!" The phrase from Marmeladov's story immediately comes to Raskolnikov's mind: " 'Do you understand, do you understand, what that purity and cleanness means?' " (I, 4)

These words lead Raskolnikov to compare Sonia's fate to Dunia's; if the latter marries Luzhin: "Do you realize that a Mrs. Luzhin's cleanness is exactly the same thing as little Sonia's, maybe even worse, nastier, fouler; because you, dear Dunia, will still have some scrap ends of comfort, while there it's a case of death from hunger!" (I, 4) Further on in this vein is the scene which Raskolnikov witnesses on the Konnogvardeysky Boulevard: a "fat dandy" intends to take advantage of a young girl who has just been made drunk and seduced. "Hey, you, Svidrigailov!" cries out Raskolnikov, directly comparing Svidrigailov's pursuit of Dunia to the pursuit of the young girl by this "fat dandy." [Chirkov at this point in his essay cites a number of other "impressions" of the same order: the episode in the police station involving the owner of a brothel (II, 1); Raskolnikov's encounter with prostitutes in the Hay Market (II, 7); the attempted suicide of a woman off Voznesensky Bridge (II, 6); Raskolnikov's meeting with a fifteen year old street singer whose dress anticipates that of Sonia (II, 6); the lewd five-year old of Svidrigailov's dream (VI, 6) —ED.]

The theme of prostitution in *Crime and Punishment* is treated quite differently from the way it is in *Notes from the Underground*—on an immeasureably broader scale and in its entire social context. Dostoevsky shows how the debasement of women and children is indigenous to the whole environment of rapacious exploitation, profiteering and speculation which forms the setting of his novel. The prostitution of young girls contains something both fascinating and fatal, forming one of the basic leitmotifs of *Crime and Punishment*. Prostitution, shown in the novel to be inseparable from the essence of capitalism, at the same time is shown to involve the desecration of a primevally pure, childlike image in man, not only in the children depicted in the novel but in all men. This image of the child in man emerges with special clarity in the person of Sonia Marmeladov.

Essential, also, for the treatment of prostitution in *Crime and Punishment* is the notion of the absence of a clear-cut, real boundary between innocence and vice. The recurrent motif just described, with its strong emotional resonances—the comparisons between Sonia and Dunia, and between the drunken girl whom Raskolnikov meets on the Konnogvardeysky Boulevard and the "dame aux camélias" in Svidrigailov's dream— have one thematic orientation: they link in a common chain what the language of moral categories calls "virtue" and "vice." A kind of tragic necessity is revealed in this contiguity, interaction, and merging of "virtue" and "vice," of childlike innocence and extreme degradation. . . .

Dostoevsky emphasizes the striking contradictions in the social life of St. Petersburg. Two kinds of impressions, mutually complementary and contradictory, occur as leitmotifs throughout the entire novel. The first is linked with the feeling of extreme confinement, with the lack of space or the need for air. Such is the impression given of Raskolnikov's room, his "ship's cabin," where his dialectic was "sharpened like a razor" and where his plan for the murder grew and matured. This room is a micro-cosm of the city as a whole. Pulcheria Alexandrovna observes: "Here and even outside it's like a room without windows." (III, 4) The novel is studded with images of confinement, stuffiness, and crowds. People, as though obeying some irresistible command, press as closely as possible to each other. They even press together while gathering around filth. On his way to kill the old woman, Raskolnikov wonders: "Why is it that in all the great cities, and not merely or exclusively because of necessity, but rather because of some special inclination, people settle and live in those parts of the city where there are neither parks nor fountains, but dirt and stench and slime of all kinds." (I, 6) But an acute sense of alienation from one another accompanies this irresistible impulse of the people in the city to crowd together, even in filth and ugliness. The extreme inner solitude of the individual contrasts sharply with the physical proximity of men to one another.

A fundamental problem in all of Dostoevsky's works, touched upon with special clarity in *Notes from the House of the Dead,* occupies a central place in *Crime and Punishment*: the antinomy of the social and anti-social in man. The murder which Raskolnikov commits is a consistent, logically inevitable act, emerging from the laws of the society in which he lives.

The moral atmosphere of Petersburg in *Crime and Punishment* is one of universal frustration, spite, and derision. Each group and each clique reacts to the misfortunes or failures of the individual man with spiteful, malicious laughter. As Marmeladov tells his story to Raskolnikov, he evokes the cruel mockery of the habitués of the local tavern; and when, trampled by horses, he is brought home, the tenants, smoking cigarettes and "disrepectfully dressed," snicker carelessly as Katerina Ivanovna squabbles with the landlady.

On the Nikolaevsky Bridge a coachman strikes Raskolnikov with his whip:

> The blow of the whip stung, and he hopped over to the parapet. He did not know why he had been walking straight down the middle, where there were vehicles and no pedestrians. He clenched and ground his teeth furiously. People around him were laughing.
> 'That'll teach him!'
> 'Sly bastard.'
> 'Sure. Pretends to be drunk, throws himself under the wheels on purpose, then you have to answer for him.'
> 'That's the way they earn a living, pal, they earn a living that way.'
> (II, 2)

It is striking to see how malicious joy over the failures or misfortunes of others will unite people and draw them closer together. Marmeladov in his confession to Raskolnikov observes: "Poverty's no vice . . . But destitution . . . is most certainly a vice. . . . When you are destitute . . . they sweep you clear of human companionship." (I, 2) For Raskolnikov this ruthless law of the society which surrounds him is more than painfully clear. Wishing at first to help the young girl who is being pursued by the "fat dandy" on the Konnogvardeysky Boulevard, Raskolnikov later rejects his original impulse. "Let them swallow each other alive— what's it to me?" (I, 4)

Dostoevsky characteristically asserts in *Crime and Punishment* that antisocial feeling is deeply instinctive in man. In describing Marmeladov's death Dostoevsky reports only his observations on the reactions of the people present, but as novelist he generalizes with respect to what he observes: "One by one the tenants crowded back to the doorway, with that strange inner feeling of satisfaction that may always be observed in the course of a sudden accident, even in those who are closest to the victim, and from which no living man is exempt, however sincere his sympathy and compassion." (II, 7)

The story of Raskolnikov's crime is the story of the maximum intensification of both social and antisocial feeling in the soul of a man. Dostoevsky emphasizes Raskolnikov's heightened social consciousness in a number of places. He is portrayed as extremely sensitive to the fate of others and to the fate of those close to him, his sister and his mother; but his sensitivity extends beyond his family. . . .

Raskolnikov possesses moral awareness in the deepest sense and represents the highest moral potential in man. . . . His sensitivity to the sufferings of others, his acute reaction to such social evils as prostitution, in a word, his heightened social consciousness are among the strongest factors leading Raskolnikov to crime. Indeed we may say that Raskolnikov's intense moral feeling and awareness—what might be called his moral maximalism—is one of the essential preconditions of his crime. But most remarkable in the novel is the fact that this depth of moral feeling and awareness is closely related to his isolation and estrangement from other men. Dostoevsky shows how Raskolnikov's high degree of moral sensitivity is accompanied by a growth of antisocial feeling in him. As early as the first chapters of the novel Dostoevsky remarks on the gloomy, morose character of his hero: "Raskolnikov had had almost no friends at the university, had felt estranged from all, went to see no one, and had been reluctant to invite anyone to come to see him." (I, 4)

Dostoevsky describes the process of Raskolnikov's growing feelings of alienation, which lead him in the end to a spiritual impasse. The conflicts which Raskolnikov experiences are agonizing: his antisocial feelings are forced to their maximum intensity at the same time that he feels the evils of society as if they were wounds in his own body. Dostoevsky takes care to map the development of this complex intellectual and emotional condition from every angle.

The intimate connection is stressed more than once in the novel between Raskolnikov's bloody "idea" and the room in which he lives. He sometimes experiences, even before the murder of the old woman and Lizaveta, a kind of eerie feeling in this room: ". . . suddenly the idea of returning home appalled him terribly. There, in his corner, in that terrible cupboard, for more than a month now, all *this* had been ripening. He walked where his eyes led him." (I, 5)

After he has committed the murder Raskolnikov senses his inner isolation for the first time in the police station: "He suddenly felt within himself a gloomy sensation of tormented, infinite solitude and estrangement. . . . Something happened inside him he had never known before, something entirely new, sudden, and unprecedented. Not that he understood it. Yet with every fiber of his being he clearly sensed not only that he would not be able to turn again as he had a little while ago, with a kind of sentimental expansiveness, to the people in the police station, but that he would never again be able to communicate with them about anything—not even if, instead of police officials, they turned out to be his blood brothers and sisters. Until that moment he had never before experienced such a strange and terrible sensation. Most painful of all, it was more a sensation than it was understanding or conscious awareness; an immediate sensation, the most painful of all the sensations he had experienced in his lifetime." (II, 1)

Simultaneously with this feeling of extreme isolation Raskolnikov experiences a surge of disgust and loathing toward everyone and everything: "With every moment a new and irresistible sensation held increasing sway over him—it was a kind of boundless, almost physical disgust —obstinate, angry, and virulent—toward everyone he met and everything around him. The people he met seemed loathsome; their faces were loathsome, their walk, their movements. If anyone had addressed him, he would have been quite capable of simply spitting on him or biting him." (II, 2) Together with his feelings of estrangement from others, Raskolnikov also senses a curious feeling of estrangement from himself, from his former self, from his former feelings and thoughts, and from his whole past. After the murder Raskolnikov looks from the Nikolaevsky Bridge onto the panorama of Petersburg and reviews his previous ideas: "In some depth below, somewhere far beneath his feet and barely discernible, stirred all the life he had lived, the thoughts he had thought, the business that had kept him busy, the subjects that had concerned him, the sights that had impressed themselves on him, and the superb view and he himself and everything, everything. . . . He seemed to be flying away somewhere, higher and higher, and everything was disappearing before his eyes." (II, 2)

After the murder Raskolnikov also undergoes a complete change of feeling toward his loved ones—his mother and sister. He says to them during a meeting: "Here you are . . . and I feel I am seeing you from a thousand miles away." Raskolnikov is fully aware of his present feelings toward his relatives: "How I loved my mother and sister! Why do I hate them now? Yes, I hate them, physically hate them. I can't bear to have them near me."

How does Raskolnikov's isolation begin? Where do the roots of his antisocial feeling lie? Is it in his personality? Yes, indisputably; but not only in his personality. To a great extent his emotional state stems from his response to the impressions he receives from the social environment around him, from objective reality. *Crime and Punishment* responds to the questions of the sources of Raskolnikov's behavior in many ways and with a number of situations, the main idea of which may be formulated in the phrase: tragic necessity. In conversation with Dunia, Raskolnikov says: "You'll reach a certain point, and if you can't go beyond it, you'll be unhappy. If you do go beyond it, though, you might even be more unhappy." Raskolnikov here is referring to himself. He recognizes the inevitable necessity of the act he has committed.

And in fact, all the most important stages Raskolnikov passes through in the novel are shown in the light of their inescapable necessity. Above all, Raskolnikov is faced with the inevitability of his conclusions on the full moral permissibility of murder, with the logical irrefutability of these conclusions, and of his idea of the "justice" of the murder of the old woman. A number of important encounters and coincidences drive Raskolnikov directly to the murder. Moreover, the theme of prostitution, which occurs, as we have noted, throughout the entire novel, is indissolubly linked with Raskolnikov's "crime."

Raskolnikov's apprehension and interpretation of prostitution is the most important point in the formation and fulfillment of his plan. According to his logic, prostitution, and in particular Sonia's plight, serves as complete justification for the murder which he has committed. Defending his "idea," Raskolnikov says to Sonia: "It's true, though, that you are a terrible sinner," he added, practically enraptured. "Mostly because you've mortified yourself and sold yourself *in vain*. There's a horror for you, a real horror. You live in this muck that you hate, and all the time you know yourself—all you have to do is open your eyes—you won't help anybody this way, you won't save anybody from anything!" (IV, 4)

Throughout the entire novel Raskolnikov is tormented by recurrent images of beating—violent beating and beating to death. These images haunt him. First, before his murder of the old woman, he dreams of a peasant beating a horse to death. Then, after the murder, he has a new dream: this time the police lieutenant, Ilya Petrovich, is beating Raskolnikov's landlady half to death. Finally, Raskolnikov relives in a dream his murder of the old woman. All of Raskolnikov's experiences, thoughts, and feelings seem to point to the fact that the supreme law of the universe and its highest imperative is murder. He commits a "murder of principle," as if obeying some kind of absolute command. Raskolnikov

learns completely by accident from Lizaveta's conversation with a mer-
chant in the Haymarket that the old woman will be alone the next day
at seven o'clock in the evening; he has a superstitious reaction: "as if
some kind of predetermined law in fact were operating here."

In describing how Raskolnikov carries out his plan for murder, Dostoevsky repeatedly and persistently stresses two points: on the one hand, there
is Raskolnikov's desperate inner resistance to what he is doing; and on
the other—the automatism inherent in his actions. These two points are
psychologically inseparable from one another. Even much later, after the
murder, Raskolnikov recognizes that he did not go to kill the old woman
"on his own legs." And earlier, describing Raskolnikov's preparations for
the murder, Dostoevsky observes: "This last day, however, which had so
unexpectedly decided everything at once, had caught him up almost automatically, as if by the hand, and pulled him along with unnatural power,
blindly, irresistibly, and with no objections on his part; and he was
caught, as if by the hem of his coat in the cog of a wheel, and being drawn
in." (I, 6)

Further on, Dostoevsky reports that as Raskolnikov approaches the act
of murder, he "ceases to believe in his own most resolute decisions" and
that everything occurs "somewhat inadvertently and even unexpectedly."
Relating in detail the scene of the murder, Dostoevsky speaks of a kind
of physical weakness in Raskolnikov, of the fact that "his mind went
blank for moments at a time, and he had almost no sense of his body."
(I, 6) At the actual moment of the murder Dostoevsky emphasizes once
more the automatism of Raskolnikov's actions: "He drew the ax out all
the way, raised it back with both hands, hardly aware of what he was
doing; and almost without effort, almost automatically, he brought the
blunt side down on her head. He seemed to have no strength. Yet the
moment he started bringing the ax down, strength sprang up in him."
(I, 7) Moreover, during the whole act we are aware of Raskolnikov's in-
surmountable aversion to what he is doing. The murder of the old woman
is depicted as an immense act of violence of Raskolnikov upon himself,
as a form of suicide. In his confession to Sonia he himself admits: "What
do you mean, *killed?* Is killing done like that? The way I did it? Some-
time I'll tell you what it was like. . . . Did I kill the old hag? No, not the
old hag—I killed myself! I went there, and all at once I did away with
myself forever! But it was the Devil who killed the old hag—not me!"
(V, 4)

The process by which Raskolnikov is exposed as the murderer and, more
important, the process of Raskolnikov's own exposure of himself occur
with the same force of necessity that drives him to commit the murder in
the first place. Dostoevsky stresses clear parallels between the "crime" and
the "punishment," between Raskolnikov's preparation for the murder
and his own exposure of himself. After he has committed the murder, we
see a sharp dichotomy between his thoughts and his actions. On the one

hand, right up to the epilogue Raskolnikov's statements and avowals testify to the fact that he does not renounce his ideas, his theory, and his logical conclusions. On the other hand, something stronger than consciousness and will—a kind of instinct—drives him on toward self-revelation. Raskolnikov himself goes to the inspector, Porfiry Petrovich, like "a moth to the flame," almost gives himself away in conversation with Zamiotov in the tavern, and goes to the empty apartment of the murdered old woman and rings the bell in order to reexperience his earlier sensations. In the scene of Raskolnikov's confession before Sonia, Dostoevsky notes that when faced with the question of whether or not to tell Sonia, Raskolnikov "felt simultaneously that not only was it impossible not to tell, but that even to postpone the moment of telling for a short time was beyond him. He did not yet know why it was beyond him; he merely *felt* it was so, and this anguished awareness of his impotence before necessity almost crushed him." (V, 4)

Raskolnikov is thus driven by necessity, a necessity which he is unable to understand even in the end. Dostoevsky stresses this point further in his subsequent construction of an analogy between the murder and the confession of guilt to Sonia. Just before Raskolnikov finally reveals to Sonia that he is Lizaveta's murderer, he again feels himself in the power of those emotions which directly controlled him at the moment of the murder. "In his awareness this moment seemed horribly like the moment he had stood behind the old woman, the ax already free of the loop, when he had felt there 'was not a moment to lose.'" (V, 4) Before going to plead guilty, Raskolnikov violently defends the conclusions of his theory to Dunia and Sonia. Yet he follows without deviation his seemingly predetermined path to self-revelation. He "pleads guilty." The novel thus stresses the aspect of tragic necessity in Raskolnikov's life and in all his actions. In a somewhat different vein, it also brings to light the deep-rooted inconsistency of the path Raskolnikov has chosen. The extreme spiritual isolation to which his own theory and its practical application lead him forces him to feel out other paths and, finally, to act contrary to his own ideas and arguments.

A perspective is introduced in *Crime and Punishment,* a point of view, which imparts a historical dimension to the action and which, as we have noted, becomes an essential component of the thematic structure of the Dostoevskian novel of the sixties and the seventies. Raskolnikov's theory and practice are illumined not only in the context of capitalism in Russia and in Petersburg in the sixties, but also in the context of that broad historical perspective which constitutes the particular background for the crime.

This historical perspective makes itself clearly felt for the first time in Raskolnikov's article "On Crime," which is a topic of discussion at Porfiry Petrovich's apartment. Raskolnikov illustrates his division of people into "ordinary" and "extraordinary" with such examples as Lycurgus, Solon,

Mohammed, and Napoleon, who "were all criminals, to a man. Even if only because they violated the old law in giving a new one—law handed down by their fathers and considered sacred by society . . . these benefactors and architects of our humanity have been for the most part especially fierce at shedding blood." (III, 5) Raskolnikov's article also names such world-famous scientists as Kepler and Newton with the idea that "Newton would have the right, he would even be obliged * * *[2] to remove these ten men, or these hundred men, so he could make his discoveries known to all mankind." (III, 5)

Figures from world history occur not only in the pages of Raskolnikov's article; they repeatedly crop up in his thoughts and his monologues and, in their own way, form one of the basic leitmotifs of the novel. The images of Napoleon and Mohammed come again to Raskolnikov's mind when he returns to his room after his encounter with the artisan who looks him in the eyes and utters solemnly: "Murderer!" And Raskolnikov refers to Napoleon once more when he is explaining to Sonia why he killed Aliona Ivanovna. Near the end of the novel, before pleading guilty, Raskolnikov responds to Dunia's observation "But you have shed blood!" with the statement: "Which they all shed . . . which cascades, and always has, down upon the earth like a waterfall, which they pour like champagne, and for which they are crowned on the Capitoline and called the benefactors of mankind." (VI, 7)

In one respect, this historical perspective imparts a tragic intensity to Raskolnikov's design: because of it, his theory in his own mind receives philosophical substantiation and takes on the aspect of historical necessity. In another respect, however, when compared with the poverty of Raskolnikov's action, this perspective has an obviously ironical ring. A completely new interpretation arises as a result of the comparison of the lives of such historical figures as Lycurgus, Mohammed and Napoleon with the murder of an insignificant old pawnbroker woman. Throughout the novel, Raskolnikov's "venture" is constantly compared to Napoleon's career, with Raskolnikov himself keenly recognizing the irony of his action: "Napoleon, the pyramids, Waterloo—that vile, skinny clerk's widow, that wizened old bag, the pawnbroker woman with the red trunk under her bed—well, how could even Porfiry Petrovich make a stew of that one!" (III, 7) Raskolnikov's entire fate in the novel is seen in the context of passionate self-affirmation, and affirmation of his "idea"—the justification of murder by conscience. It is at the same time seen in the context of a no less sweeping self-negation. Raskolnikov's ironical view of his "undertaking" is one of the instances of this self-negation.

The grouping of the characters as well as Raskolnikov's relationship with them must be examined in order to understand the meaning of the

---

[2] [Dostoevsky's original ellipses have been replaced by asterisks. Ellipses in this article indicate my deletions. ED.]

novel as a whole. To begin with, there is the important relationship of Raskolnikov and Katerina Ivanovna, who, because of her whole moral outlook, must be placed beside Raskolnikov. Her "truth" is different from Sonia's "truth" and akin to Raskolnikov's "truth." Katerina Ivanovna is a woman who demands justice, justice at all costs, and at once, now. Sonia describes her stepmother in this way: "She looks for what's right * * * She's pure. She has such faith that there must be a 'right' in everything, and she makes demands * * *. Even if you tortured her she wouldn't do what wasn't right. She doesn't know it's not possible for people to do 'right' to each other so she gets upset." (IV, 4)

But Raskolnikov, too, demands justice and appeals to it in the dialogues with Sonia. He feels that suicide in Sonia's position is "more just, a thousand times more just" than her life, and in the three meetings with her he feverishly argues the correctness of his idea. His entire argument is directed at proving one thing: that the way out he proposes is the only just one. Katerina Ivanovna lives in the illusion of an imminent and decisive revolution in her life: help will come from somewhere; they will move to another city, and she will be the superintendent of a boarding house. In her view, all was unjust but in the future all will be just. Raskolnikov, however, intends to effect an instantaneous and radical revolution in the social-historical world order. To Sonia's question, "But what can be done? What can be done?" in his first meeting with her, Raskolnikov replies: "What can be done? Smash what has to be smashed, once and for all—that's all there is to it; and take the suffering on oneself! What, you don't understand? You'll understand later * * *. Freedom and power, but the main thing is power! Over all trembling flesh and over the whole ant heap! * * * That's the goal! Remember that! Those are my parting words to you!" (IV, 4) Idealistic philosophy proposes the idea of a moral world order. Raskolnikov denies this idea yet acts in the name of his own categorical moral imperatives. He wants to effect an original world revolution, a Copernican revolution with his idea of the "moral permission to shed blood," "bloodshed in the name of conscience."

Katerina Ivanovna and Raskolnikov in their obsessive pride are individuals with a strong sense of wounded personal identity. Raskolnikov is a theomachist. True, he replies that he believes in God to Porfiry Petrovich's direct question. But in private conversation with Sonia he remarks to her "with a kind of malicious enjoyment": "And perhaps God does not exist." Declaring war on the entire world order, violating the commandment "Thou shall not kill," and proclaiming a new law of the universe—the moral right to kill, Raskolnikov treads the soil of metaphysical rebellion. Katerina Ivanovna in her own way, too, is a rebel and theomachist. The difference between her death and the deaths of all other Dostoevskian heroes is striking. Dying, she will not agree to the proposal to summon a priest: "What? A priest? Don't need him * * * where did the money come from? I don't have any sins! God has to forgive me anyway * * *. He knows how I've suffered. * * * And if he won't forgive me, what difference will a priest make!" (V, 5) One is amazed to find in the ruined life of such a fragile and, it would seem, infinitely weak creature such courage and relentless pride.

Particularly important for an understanding of the entire ideological conception of *Crime and Punishment* is the antithesis of Raskolnikov and Svidrigailov. The life and fate of Raskolnikov are characterized by a "non-acceptance of the world," a principled battle against the world order; the life and fate of Svidrigailov, by an overacceptance, by a complete acquiescence to everything, good and evil, a kind of principled nonresistance to existence in all its aspects.

The social biography of Svidrigailov is typical, bearing a manifest similarity to the biography of Prince Valkovsky in *The Insulted and Injured,* with its strong emphasis on the traits of the declassé nobleman. The portly nobleman of the patriarchal serf-owning structure who allows his hand to be kissed in a tavern, the inveterate voluptuary, the landowner in the midst of the filth of the dens of St. Petersburg, Svidrigailov in every aspect is a "man of the past." His whole life, reflecting the process of the degradation of the nobility, destines Svidrigailov for a knowledge of people on the most diverse levels of the social ladder, down to the most abjectly poverty-stricken dregs of the city. And thus Svidrigailov, with all his depravity, is bathed in an atmosphere of peculiar wisdom. Concerned with the affair of the "brutal and, so to speak, fantastic murder," guilty of the rape of a young girl, guilty of the suicide of his servant, Filipp, evidently responsible for the death of his wife, Marfa Petrovna, Svidrigailov can, from a distance, sense in Raskolnikov his own kind of man, that they are birds of a feather, "berries from the same tree." He instinctively detects Raskolnikov's "crime," sets himself up as his shadow, and uncovers his secret. Svidrigailov's amoralism is sharply delineated; to possess Dunia he would do anything. His consistent amoralism is in contrast to Raskolnikov's frenzied moralism. The antithesis of Valkovsky and Ivan Petrovich in *The Insulted and Injured* is repeated here in a new form, and the name of Schiller again appears on the scene as a symbol of ethical idealism. Svidrigailov ridicules the Schiller in Raskolnikov.

But the "man of the past" can, in addition, understand and properly assess Raskolnikov's theory. Svidrigailov repeats this theory to Dunia in irony: "We have here also some sort of personal theory of his own—not such a bad theory—by which people are divided, you see, into those who are raw material and those who are special people. I mean, those who are so lofty the law was not written for them, but on the contrary, they themselves make the law for the other people, the raw material, the garbage. It's not such a bad theory, nothing special; *une théorie comme une autre.*" (VI, 5)

Svidrigailov, however, is capable of completely understanding not only Raskolnikov but also Sonia and the other characters, and in this way the "man-universe" appears again in Dostoevsky in another form.[3] In Svidrigailov the "multiplicity of feelings" of the "underground man" is revived, and, like the "underground man," Svidrigailov is capable of infinite awareness, with a capacity to combine in his thoughts and actions the most extreme contradictions. Svidrigailov, a man who in the past seduced a young girl, causing her to commit suicide, in his own words "loves children." He contemplates suicide and relentlessly, inflamed with passion, pursues Dunia yet at the same time intends to marry another. He has a young fiancée; he makes her sit on his lap and brings her to tears with his unceremonious caresses. This same Svidrigailov, however, enters most intimately into the fate of the Marmeladov family, contributes to the support of its orphaned children, sincerely helps Sonia, refuses marriage, and provides for the future of his young fiancée.

The more depraved Svidrigailov is, the more unbridled his powerful bursts of passion, the more difficult it is for him to control himself. His rejection by Dunia puts him under the greatest emotional strain, and a battle within himself against his own intense reactions ensues. Dostoevsky emphasizes this. Svidrigailov lures Dunia into his room, where she threatens to shoot him, then unexpectedly drops the gun. "Something seemed to lift from his heart, and it may not only have been the weight of his fear of death; he seemed at the moment scarcely even aware of that. It was release from a more melancholy and more somber feeling, which even he himself could not have fully defined." (VI, 5) Before releasing Dunia, Svidrigailov, in Dostoevsky's words, undergoes the following experience: "For a moment a terrible, mute struggle took place in the soul of Svidrigailov. He looked at her somehow in a way that was beyond words. Suddenly he removed his arm, turned around, strode quickly to the window, and stood there in front of it." (VI, 5) We thus witness the supreme moral act—a man's victory over himself. But Svidrigailov surprises us with more than this act of renunciation and magnanimity. He also is seen to possess a deep, sincere sympathy for all those whom life

[3] "Man-universe": a literal rendering of Chirkov's *"chelovek-univers,"* that is, man as a universe in miniature, as microcosm. As early as *Notes from the House of the Dead,* Chirkov asserts, Dostoevsky gives expression to a conception of man which will dominate his later philosophical novels—the conception of the "man-universe." "Man possesses the capacity for unprecedented degradation and perversion," explains Chirkov, "and the capacity for moral renewal and infinite perfection. He has the capacity for the most diverse and contradictory actions, a capacity for everything—both good and evil. Man is a universe in miniature—a universe in compressed form." Dostoevsky's man from the "underground" is a caricature of the "man-universe." In Prince Myshkin (*The Idiot*), Chirkov maintains, Dostoevsky depicts the same psychological phenomena which he depicted in the man from the "underground" and in Svidrigailov. Myshkin, like Svidrigailov, judges no one. But at the same time, Dostoevsky's image of Myshkin is a new phase of the "man-universe," one to which Dostoevsky positively responds. Unlike Svidrigailov, there is no nonresistance to life in Myshkin, but a sympathy for all, and above all, a sensitivity to the suffering of others." (See N. M. Chirkov's, *O stile Dostoevskogo* [Moscow, 1967], pp. 25, 51, 143.)

wounds and passes over in silence. He roams the whole "cesspool" that is Petersburg; poor people surround him—street singers, lackeys, waiters. He is drawn to them. By what force? Idleness and the desire somehow to fill the infinite emptiness of his life? No; rather it is the unquestionable need to come to know and to try everything, to experience the broadest range of feelings and sensations.

Svidrigailov has still one more important trait which is later characteristic of the true Dostoevskian hero (Myshkin, Aliosha). Svidrigailov declares to Dunia: "You know, in general, how I think; I make it a rule to condemn absolutely nobody." He does not even condemn Raskolnikov. He allows everything and judges nothing. We note in this connection that one of the basic traits of Aliosha Karamazov, which impresses even Fiodor Pavlovich, is that Aliosha judges no one. Svidrigailov is also a distinctive "man-universe," in the sense that he possesses an unlimited capacity for vice, an absolute nonresistance, and even submission, to evil, and at the same time a capacity for the highest moral order, with a limitless ability to seek out the good. He is a man, he says, and nothing human is foreign to him. He is allowed the whole range of human experiences, feelings, and actions.

Svidrigailov is a character with deep social and historical significance. "Russians, in general," he says to Dunia during their last meeting, "are people of a certain breadth. They are broad like their land, and they are exceptionally strongly drawn to the fantastic and the disorderly. But the trouble consists in being broad without any special genius . . . As you know, Avdotia Romanovna, we don't have any especially sacred traditions in our educated society; it's as if somebody patched something together the best he could out of books, one way or another, or extracted it out of the ancient chronicles." (VI, 5) We find ideas similar to these of Svidrigailov on social-historical questions in Dostoevsky's subsequent novels and in *The Diary of a Writer*.

Svidrigailov provides a clear illustration of how the "educated class," as Dostoevsky conceives it, is lacking in social-historical foundations. Svidrigailov is cut off from any deep social-historical roots. By the whole stamp of his personality he has little in common with the landowning nobility, yet at the same time he has no links whatever with the popular masses. He moves in a social vacuum. Svidrigailov serves to illustrate Dostoevsky's idea that the "educated class" has been alienated from the people since the time of the reforms of Peter I, and that the rapid surge of capitalism into Russian life after 1861 revealed this alienation in all its depth. The "multiplicity of feelings" in Svidrigailov, his capacity for everything, both good and evil, is at the same time his total indifference to everything, his complete spiritual emptiness, his irremediable melancholy and apathy (because of which he is even ready, he says, to fly off with Berg in a balloon), his absolute skepticism and nihilism—all these, after the last strong emotional attraction (Dunia) is lost to him—lead Svidrigailov inevitably to suicide. A "concurrence of extremes" in his personality brings Svidrigailov, like the "underground man," to spiritual destruction.

The antithesis of Raskolnikov and the police inspector, Porfiry Petrovich, is of great significance to the ideological conception of *Crime and Punishment*. Like Svidrigailov, Porfiry Petrovich is depicted as a man of exceptional awareness and intuition. In his role as investigator, the inspector immediately hits the mark in exposing Raskolnikov as the murderer. But Porfiry Petrovich is more than a clever and astute investigator. He is also shown to be a man with a deep knowledge of life. He not only immediately surmises that Raskolnikov is the murderer but also discerns Raskolnikov's personality and perceives his private thoughts and impulses. Long before the murder his attention is drawn to Raskolnikov's article, "On Crime," and in his last meeting with him Porfiry Petrovich expresses a penetrating understanding of Raskolnikov's emotional state when he wrote the article. Porfiry Petrovich says to Raskolnikov:

> You are bold, proud and serious, and you have been through a great deal, you've been through a great deal, I knew that all long ago. I am familiar with all these moods, and as I read it, your little essay seemed quite familiar. It was thought out on sleepless nights and in a state of wild excitement, heart heaving and pounding, and with suppressed enthusiasm. It's dangerous, though—this proud, suppressed enthusiasm in a young man! I jeered at you at the time, but I'll tell you now that I'm terribly fond—I mean as an admirer—of this first, youthful, passionate experimenting with the pen. Smoke—mist—a chord sounds in the mist. Your essay's absurd and fantastic, but there's such a sincerity keeps flashing through it, such a youthful, incorruptible pride, such desperate boldness; and it's rather somber, your essay; well, but that's to the good, yes. (VI, 2)

Porfiry Petrovich speaks here as if he were very familiar if not with Raskolnikov's act, that of murder, at least with the emotional experiences and the inner motives which drove Raskolnikov to commit murder. The inspector understands Raskolnikov because he senses in himself the capacity for a similar act. Like Svidrigailov, Porfiry Petrovich is capable of deep feeling and therefore of deep understanding. He is an all-comprehending man, and the "man-universe" also lives in him. Porfiry Petrovich is an extremely important character because he is chosen by Dostoevsky to be the spokesman of one of the main ideas of the novel. The inspector says to Raskolnikov at the end of his last conversation with him: "I tell you I'm even convinced you would 'bring yourself to accept suffering.' You don't have to take my word for it now, but dwell on it. Suffering is a great thing, Rodion Romanych; don't be blinded by the fact that I've grown fat, because I know—don't laugh—there is an idea in suffering. Mikolka's right, you know." (VI, 2)

The inspector, however, not only expresses Dostoevsky's idea of suffering; even more important is his expression of Dostoevsky's idea of life, and

in this lies the true thematic core of the novel. A passionate love of life
is a basic *leitmotif* running through the entire work. When Raskolnikov
meets the prostitutes at the entrance of the tavern in the Haymarket and
his thoughts turn to the meaning of life ("constructing one's whole life
on a square yard of space for a thousand years, through all eternity"), he
cries out: "It would still be better to live like that than die at the moment.
To live and to live and to live and to live! No matter how you live, if
only to live! How true that is! God, how true! What a scoundrel man is!
And he's a scoundrel who calls him a scoundrel for that," he added a
minute later. (II, 6)

Raskolnikov's expression of such an inscrutable, irrational love of life
with all the monstrous and crushing contradictions that life has had for
him seems in itself, however, like a kind of madness. Porfiry Petrovich has
a different conception of this power of life: "I know it's hard to believe,"
he says to Lizaveta's murderer, "but give yourself up to life directly,
without sophistry; don't puzzle over it. Don't worry. It will carry you
straight to shore and set you on your feet. What shore? How should I
know! I only believe you still have a lot for which to live." (VI, 2) And
further on Porfiry Petrovich again repeats, "Do what justice demands. I
know you don't believe it—but, by God, life will sustain you. Later you'll
accept yourself again. Air is what you need now—air, air!" (VI, 2)

The relationship of Raskolnikov and Dunia—of brother and sister—is
also important to the development of the ideological conception of the
novel. They mutually complement and characterize one another. Two
parallel places in the text of the novel are of interest. In conversation
with Raskolnikov, Svidrigailov describes Dunia's character this way: "You
know, from the very beginning, I thought it was a pity fate hadn't ar-
ranged for your sister to be born in the second or third century of our
era, the daughter of some local ruler or a proconsul in Asia Minor. No
doubt she would have been among the martyrs; and when they seared her
breast with red-hot irons, she would no doubt have smiled. She'd have deliberately chosen that path; and in the fourth or fifth centuries she would
have gone out into the Egyptian desert and lived there thirty years, on
roots, ecstasies, and visions. That's all she thirsts for; she asks to take
someone else's suffering upon herself, and right away! And if she can't
she'll throw herself out the window!" (VI, 4) And Porfiry Petrovich says
to Raskolnikov: "You want to know the kind of man I think you are? I
think you're the kind of man who would stand there and smile at his
torturers while they were tearing out his guts—if only he could find faith
or a god." (VI, 2)

We find the similarity of brother and sister accentuated in their basic
personality traits, and this similarity has its ideological and thematic
function for the novel's artistic objective: to emphasize the pathos of the
asceticism characteristic of both Raskolnikovs, brother and sister. Raskolnikov's path shows the passage of a criminal to an ascetic. His tre-

mendous potential force is particularly emphasized in the novel. Thus, Porfiry Petrovich says of him: "Mr. Zamiotov was the first to be struck by your anger and your open daring. Well, I mean, suddenly blurting it out in a tavern—'I killed her!'—just like that! Too daring, yes, too bold; and if it should be he's guilty, I thought, then he's a hard fighter!" (VI, 2)

Of exceptional significance in the novel is the relationship between Raskolnikov and the Marmeladovs, the father and especially Sonia. Through this relationship the theme of the gospel is introduced. Raskolnikov, Marmeladov, and Sonia form a distinctive triad—a triad which suggests the gospel images of the criminal, the outcast, and the harlot.

The theme of Marmeladov is that of the one who is accursed, but in a new sociological and psychological version: the Petersburg drunkard, the petty bureaucrat of the mid-nineteenth century as an outcast. Marmeladov reveals an agonizing consciousness of his infinite guilt before his family, and especially before Sonia, a merciless self-condemnation, and an impulse to ascend from the depths of the worst degradation to the light and the good.

The theme of Sonia is not only that of self-condemnation, but especially that of infinite self-renunciation, a willingness for the sake of her relatives and for others to accept utter disgrace and the most extreme humiliation—the selling of her body—and to sharing with a murderer his life's path. The meeting of Raskolnikov and Sonia is as much an ideological key to the novel as are Porfiry Petrovich's last words to Raskolnikov. Dostoevsky's emphasis on comparing the fates of Raskolnikov and Sonia has been noted time and again. The important description of their first meeting is given as follows: "The candle end had long been flickering out in its crooked holder, dimly illuminating in this beggarly room the murderer and the harlot, who had so strangely come together here to read the Eternal Book." (IV, 4) And further on Raskolnikov says: "We're both damned, so let's go together. . . . You, too, have transgressed . . . you found within yourself you were able to transgress. You laid hands on yourself, you took a life * * * your *own*—what's the difference!" (IV, 4)

Indeed there is the deepest consonance in the fates of these two, and in this consonance lies the ultimate meaning of the novel. Raskolnikov resorts to murder because of his extreme sensitivity to the suffering of others and above all to the suffering of his relatives. Sonia, because of the same sensitivity, becomes a prostitute. But Raskolnikov is driven to murder through extreme self-assertion; Sonia, to prostitution through extreme self-negation.

Sonia's reading of the chapters from the gospel on the resurrection of Lazarus from the dead is the ultimate paradigm of Raskolnikov's fate and the point of convergence for those of the different characters and for the various threads of the novel. Its main idea is the concept of the ultimate spiritual regeneration of its hero; but at the same time it is also the concept which Porfiry Petrovich formulates in his last meeting with Raskolnikov, the concept of the invincible power of life. The novel concludes with a hymn to this power of life: the epilogue speaks of Raskolnikov's regeneration and of the new life which will begin for him.

Sonia, moreover, possesses still another important trait—one that constitutes the transition to the image of the character, Mikolka. In the epilogue Dostoevsky mentions that the prisoners did not like Raskolnikov and were once even ready to kill him. They didn't like him because of his excessive pride and the distance he maintained from them, even in prison. By way of contrast, Sonia is extremely well-liked by everyone. "Sofia Semyonovna, ma'am, you're our tender, aching mother!" So spoke these coarse, branded convicts to this tiny, skinny creature.

The thematic line to the earth and to the people originates in Sonia; it is here that we find the keystone of Dostoevsky's world view. To Dostoevsky the idea of the earth is inseparable from the idea of the people and the motherland. The earth, the people, and the motherland are for him an indissoluble ideological complex. After Raskolnikov's confession of the murder of the old pawnbroker woman and Lizaveta, Sonia gives him the inviolable order: " 'Rise!' She seized him by the shoulder. He raised himself, looking at her almost in amazement. 'Go now. Go this very moment, and stand at the crossroads; bow down, and first kiss the earth which you have defiled; then bow down to the whole world, to the four points of the compass, and say aloud, for all men to hear—I have killed!' " (V, 4) After his meeting with Sonia and immediately before giving himself up to the police, Raskolnikov goes to the Haymarket and carries out Sonia's order to the letter. Significant is the description of this act of repentance of the murderer before mother earth. "As he remembered [Sonia's words—N. Chirkov], he shook all over. The blind melancholy and anxiety of the recent past, but especially of the last few hours, oppressed him to such a degree that he simply plunged into the possibility of this new, whole, and complete sensation. It came upon him suddenly like a kind of nervous fit; took fire first as a single spark in his soul, and suddenly, like flame, seized everything. Everything seemed to melt inside him, and tears flowed. He dropped to the earth where he stood * * * " (VI, 8)

Contact with the earth and repentance before it signify for Dostoevsky a return to a whole and integrated life. The order for atonement of guilt before the earth originates from Sonia, and it is Sonia, too, who in prison preserves a vital link with the masses. Raskolnikov's rebirth is effected not only through repentance before the earth but also through the restoration of an organic link with the people as a result of his acceptance of Sonia's "truth."

Lastly, the relationship of Raskolnikov and Mikolka is very important for an understanding of the meaning of the novel. The house painter Mikolka is not a secondary figure, but a character of tremendous symbolic significance. How is he depicted? After the murder Raskolnikov goes down the stairway tense with fear and hears: " 'Hey, you bastard, you goblin, you devil! Hold up there!' With a yell someone burst out of one of the apartments below, and not only ran but practically fell downstairs, shouting loudly: 'Mitka! Mitka! Mitka! Mitka! Mitka! You fool, blast you!' " (I, 7) Relating to Zosimov with some irritation how Mikolka came to assume responsibility for the murder, Razumikhin cites the words of Mikolka's own testimony: " 'So I grabbed Mitka by the hair and I knocked him down and I was giving it to him, when Mitka, he came out from under me and grabbed my hair and started giving it to me. We weren't really mad, though. It was all in fun.' " (II, 4) Finally, Porfiry Petrovich in his last meeting with Raskolnikov describes Mikolka to him in this way:

> First he's immature, still a child; and not that he's a coward, but sensitive, a kind of artist type. Yes, really. You mustn't laugh at me for explaining him like that. He is innocent and completely impressionable. He has feelings; he is a fantast. He can sing and dance, and they say he can tell stories so people gather from all around to listen. And he'll go to school and he'll laugh himself silly because somebody somehow crooked a finger at him; and he'll drink himself senseless, not because he's a drunkard, but just every now and then, when people buy him drinks; he's like a child still. (VI, 2)

Mikolka is always presented to the reader in this way—in bursts of revelry and mirth. Mikolka is life itself in its untouched, fresh, pure, almost childlike form, life with its turbulent, varied, creative possibilities. Dostoevsky's idea consists in the fact that Mikolka, a grown man and at the same time a child, a Russian country lad capable of limitless merriment and daring, conceals a capacity for limitless self-abnegation and deeds of great heroism. Mikolka takes Raskolnikov's guilt upon himself, and Porfiry Petrovich refers precisely to Mikolka as the prototype of the future Raskolnikov. Porfiry Petrovich says to Raskolnikov: "I am even convinced you would 'bring yourself to accept suffering.' Mikolka's right, you know." (VI, 2) For Dostoevsky, Mikolka is also the "man-universe" but, in contrast to Svidrigailov, he is firmly bound to the earth and the people. Mikolka finds his roots as a character in the *Notes from the House of the Dead* (see the prisoner who comes at the guard with a brick, not to harm him, only to "find suffering" [I, 2 ED.]).

Crime and Punishment is a topical novel, imprinting on its characters the social and historical reality of Russia in the sixth decade of the nineteenth century. The relevance of the events in the novel is emphasized by Porfiry Petrovich. He speaks of Raskolnikov's crime in this way: "This is a fantastic, a somber case—contemporary, an incident of our time, yes, when the heart of man has grown dark; when you hear people cite the phrase, 'blood refreshes'; when the whole meaning of life is expounded in terms of comfort." (VI, 2) The injustices of capitalism, which color all the situations surrounding the action of the novel, are, in Dostoevsky's mind, inseparable from the breakdown of the whole moral framework of Russian life. Raskolnikov's crime is for Dostoevsky a manifestation of spiritual decay reflecting Russia's deepening social crisis in the post-reform period.

The contemporary relevance of *Crime and Punishment* is manifested in its polemical aspects. Describing the Petersburg of the 1860s, Dostoevsky could not help expressing his own unfortunately reactionary political attitude to the social movements in Russia at that time. Dostoevsky polemicizes with the ideas of socialism, and especially with those of N. G. Chernyshevsky, throughout the entire novel. This is apparent for the first time in the character Razumikhin. In discussing the question of crime at Porfiry Petrovich's, Razumikhin sets forth "the socialist point of view" in polemical tone, reducing this point of view to a mechanistic conception of environment. Raskolnikov himself speaks of the socialists with frank sarcasm: "Why did that fool Razumikhin abuse the socialists a little while ago? A diligent, industrious lot, concerned with 'universal happiness' * * * So, life is given to me but once, and I will not have it again. I don't want to wait for 'universal happiness.' I want to live myself, or better not to live at all. And so? I just didn't want to pass my hungry mother by, clutching my ruble in my pocket while I waited for 'universal happiness.' I'm carrying my little brick, so to speak, for universal happiness, and that's why my heart is at peace. Ha-ha!" (III, 6)

Dostoevsky finds other ways to polemicize with the socialists, for example, through Lebeziatnikov, an advocate of "socialist" ideas; he also tries to discredit socialism through Luzhin's arguments. Luzhin, a bourgeois opportunist, under the pretense of agreeing with Chernyshevsky's ideas of rationalism egoism, renders them absurd. In the depiction of these two characters the future author of *The Devils* is wholly in evidence. Dostoevsky often parodies subjects he wishes to expose. Various antiscientific, petty bourgeois interpretations of the ideas of the sixties find expression in Lebeziatnikov's muddled and poorly expressed arguments, for example, his vulgarized conception of the socialists' plans for the future of society and of their theory of free conjugal unions, together with a primitively utilitarian understanding of the socialist idea of art (e.g., cleaning cesspools is more important than the works of Raphael and Pushkin). Lebeziatnikov's arguments also parody the socialists' enthusiasm for the natural sciences and, in particular, for physiological theories (e.g., his explanation of the causes for Katerina Ivanovna's madness). . . .

Of course, this purely topical and journalistic side of the novel does not overshadow its tremendous ideological significance, which goes far beyond the 1860s. Dostoevsky treats the problem of crime in depth—in terms of the problem of [moral] norms, responsibility, and atonement. . . .

Each of the characters, passing through crime, bears his own punishment. Raskolnikov, in nightmares, reexperiences several times the murder he has committed. And at the moment of his confession to Sonia he sees in her face Lizaveta's face as he struck her with the ax. Svidrigailov, on the night of his own suicide, recalls, to the accompaniment of the rain and the wind, the young girl he saw commit suicide, her cursed cry that went unheard in the gloomy night, "in the damp thaw, while the wind howled." Marmeladov, before dying, sees Sonia appear at his bedside dressed as a street walker. And, like Marmeladov, Katerina Ivanovna also has her own tragic guilt, her nemesis: it was she who drove Sonia out onto the street. Katerina Ivanovna dies in Sonia's room, in the same room where the latter "receives her guests."

The first conclusion which may be drawn from these comparisons and from these various types of crime is that the boundaries of crime are difficult to define. At the same time, however, Dostoevsky consistently sets forth clear instances of guilt and responsibility. The entirely innocent Mikolka is ready to take another's guilt upon himself and to "accept suffering." The deepest roots of human conduct are so intertwined that it is difficult precisely to define the limits of the "crime" of an individual; however, the moral responsibility of each man is not thereby reduced, but vastly increased. This is Dostoevsky's second conclusion.

In Dostoevsky's mind, life in its most profound sense is expressed in the relationship of Raskolnikov and Sonia and in their mutual feeling for each other. This feeling is not without internal contradiction. Raskolnikov first hears about Sonia from Marmeladov's story, which strengthens his resolution to carry out his crime. After the murder, Raskolnikov feels that he has been cut off as if by a knife from all men and contemplates suicide or giving himself up to the police. At this point he encounters Sonia for the first time at the bedside of the dying Marmeladov and is overcome with violent emotion. (II, 7) Dostoevsky does not indicate the precise cause of this emotion. Yet Raskolnikov now feels that "life has not yet died . . . with the old woman." He experiences a tremendous feeling for life. This surge of feeling for life has only one explanation: Raskolnikov's total spiritual isolation is breaking down. The perspective of contact with another human being, of union with Sonia, opens up for him. He sees the possibility of a full experience of life with another "outcast." His meeting with Sonia in private, however, brings to the surface all that divides them. The more closely they are drawn to one another, the more fierce the battle between them. Each tries to affirm his own point of view, his "truth." Raskolnikov feels the imperative need to confess to Sonia his murder of the old woman and Lizaveta, to put his feeling for her to the test; it is an impulse in which the depths of Raskolnikov's antisocial feeling are inevitably expressed. Before his confession to Sonia "a strange, unexpected feeling of burning hatred for her suddenly passed through his heart."

The love-hate motif, occurring throughout all of Dostoevsky's works, appears once again on the pages of *Crime and Punishment*. Raskolnikov's love for Sonia arises as if through its own negation. Characteristically, even when he is in prison we see Raskolnikov's alienation from Sonia in conjunction with his alienation from the masses of prisoners. We observe the last great change in Raskolnikov after his illness in prison: the kindling in him of genuine feeling for Sonia, the surge of sincere love, which signifies the beginning of his regeneration. This release and this renewal represent a victory of life in its highest sense—the life which Dostoevsky himself continuously affirms.

The Problem of Evil

by Nicholas Berdyaev

The problem of evil and crime in Dostoevsky's work is linked with the problem of freedom. Evil is unexplainable without freedom. Wherever there is freedom there is evil. Without this link with freedom there would be no responsibility for evil. Without freedom for evil God would be responsible. Dostoevsky understood more deeply than anybody that evil is the child of freedom. But he understood also that without freedom there is no good. Good is also the child of freedom. Here is the mystery of life, the mystery of human fate. Freedom is irrational and therefore it can produce both good and evil. But to reject freedom on the grounds that it can engender evil means to engender even greater evil. For only the good that is free is good, whereas compulsion and slavery, which tempt virtue, are the evil of the anti-Christ. Here gather all the enigmas, antinomies and mysteries. Dostoevsky not only confronts us with these enigmas, but does much to resolve them. His conception of evil was very original and unique, one that leads many people astray; so one must fully understand how he posed and resolved the problem of evil. The path of freedom turns into self-will; self-will leads to evil—evil to crime. The problem of crime occupies a central place in Dostoevsky's work. He is not only an anthropologist, but an original criminologist as well. The study of the limits and boundaries of human nature leads to the study of the nature of crime. In crime man crosses these limits and boundaries. Hence the extraordinary interest in crime. What fate is experienced by the man who steps over the boundaries of the permissible? what regenerations occur as a result? Dostoevsky discloses the ontological consequences of crime. And thus it turns out that freedom, turning into self-will, leads to evil; evil to crime; crime—ineluctably and from within—to punishment. Punishment tracks man in the very depths of his own nature. . . .

"The Problem of Evil" [Editor's title]. From the chapter "Zlo" ["Evil"], in Mirosozertsanie Dostoevskogo [Dostoevsky's World Outlook], by Nikolaj Berdjaev. Copyright 1923 by the YMCA Press (Paris), pp. 88–89; 91–100. Translated from the Russian by Robert Louis Jackson. Reprinted by permission of the publishers. An English translation from the French version (L'Esprit de Dostoïevsky) of Berdjaev's work appeared in 1934. The excerpt translated here, from the original Russian, strives to remain faithful to the unique, at times redundant, but always terse and staccato style of the Russian philosopher. [ED.]

Dostoevsky's conception of evil was deeply antinomian. And the complexity of this conception has caused some people to doubt that his was a Christian one. One thing is certain: Dostoevsky does not approach evil from the juridical point of view. He wanted to *know evil,* and in this he was a gnostic. Evil is evil. The nature of evil is interior, metaphysical, and not external, social. Man as a free being is responsible for evil. Evil must be exposed in its nothingness and must be consumed in flames. And Dostoevsky passionately exposes evil and puts it to flame. This is one aspect of his conception of evil. But evil is also the path of man, his tragic path, the fate of one who is free, an experience which can also enrich man, raise him to a higher plane. But there is also another aspect to Dostoevsky's conception of evil: the immanent comprehension of evil. This is the way free people, not slaves, experience evil. The immanent experience of evil exposes its nothingness; in this experience evil is consumed and man reaches the light. But this truth is dangerous; it exists for the genuinely free and the spiritually mature. It must be hidden from the immature. And that is why Dostoevsky may appear to be a dangerous writer: because he must be read in an atmosphere of spiritual emancipation. Yet nonetheless one must admit that no writer has fought so furiously against evil and darkness as has Dostoevsky. The catechistic morality of the law cannot be an answer to the suffering of those of his heroes who embark on the path of evil. Evil is not punished from without, but has irreversible inner consequences. Legal punishment for a crime is only the inner fate of the criminal. Everything external is only the sign of the internal. The pangs of conscience are more terrible to a man than the external punishment from the law of the state. And a man brought down by the pangs of conscience awaits punishment as a relief from his agony. The law of the state—this "cold monster"—is incommensurable with the human soul. In the preliminary investigation and trial of Mitia Karamazov, Dostoevsky exposes the injustice of state law. The human soul has more meaning for him than all the kingdoms of the world. In this respect he was a Christian to his roots. But the soul itself seeks the sword of the state, of its own volition bends to its blows. The punishment is a moment on its inner journey.

Only a slave or immature person could deduce from Dostoevsky's thesis on evil that one must take the path of evil so as to obtain new experience and thus enrich oneself. One cannot make Dostoevsky the basis for an evolutionary theory of evil according to which evil is only a moment in the evolution of good. Such evolutionary optimism, defended by many theosophists, is completely contrary to Dostoevsky's tragic spirit. Least of all was he an evolutionist for whom evil is the dearth of good or a stage in the development of good. Evil for him was evil. Evil must burn in the fires of hell. And he leads evil through this hellish fire. No childish games or cunning play with evil are allowed. It is madness to think that a man could consciously embark on a course of evil with the purpose of deriving as much satisfaction from it as possible, and then give himself over energetically to the advancement of the good. This is a thoroughly despicable state of consciousness. Such argumentation cannot be taken seriously. Granted that the tragic experience of evil enriches the spiritual world of man, deepens his knowledge. Granted that there is no return to the more elementary state that precedes this experience of evil. But when the person who embarks on a course of evil, who experiences evil, begins to think that evil is enriching him and that evil is only a moment [in the development] of good, a stage in his ascension, then that person really is sinking down lower, disintegrating and perishing, turning off from the path that leads to enrichment and ascension. Such a person can learn nothing from the experience of evil, is no longer capable of transcending himself. Only through the exposure of evil, only through great suffering from evil can man be raised to great heights. Self-satisfaction in evil spells ruin. And Dostoevsky shows what pain a soul undergoes from evil and how the soul itself exposes the evil within. Evil is the tragic path of man, the fate of man, the ordeal of human freedom. But evil is not a necessary stage in the evolution of good. Evil is antinomian. And an optimistic-evolutionary understanding of evil constitutes a rationalistic voiding of this antinomy. One can profit from the experience of evil, heighten one's consciousness, but one must first pass through suffering, experience the horror of catastrophe; one must expose evil, plunge it into hellish fire, expiate one's guilt. Evil is linked with suffering and must lead to expiation. Dostoevsky believes in the expiatory and regenerative power of suffering. Life for him is first of all the expiation of guilt through suffering. Therefore, freedom is inevitably linked with expiation. Freedom led man onto the path of evil. Evil was the ordeal of freedom. Now evil must lead to expiation. In evil, engendered by freedom, freedom perishes, turns into its opposite. Expiation restores the freedom of man, returns to him his freedom. Therefore is Christ-the-Savior freedom itself. In all his novels Dostoevsky leads man through this spiritual process, through freedom, evil and expiation. He depicts the elder Zosima and Aliosha as people who have known evil and arrived at a higher state. The Karamazov element is to be found in Aliosha, and both his brother Ivan and Grushenka remark on it. He feels it within him. Aliosha, in Dostoevsky's conception, was supposed to be a person who passed through the ordeal of freedom. That was how Dostoevsky understood the fate of man.

The problem of crime is the problem of whether everything is permissible. Is everything permissible? This theme always tormented Dostoevsky; it presented itself to him ever in new forms. This is the theme of *Crime and Punishment,* but also, to a considerable degree, of *The Possessed* and *The Brothers Karamazov.* This theme is posed as the ordeal of human freedom. When man set out on the path of freedom he was faced with the question: were there any moral limits in his nature, could he dare to do anything? Freedom, becoming self-will, no longer wants to know any sanctities, any limits. If there is no God, if man himself is god, then all is permissible. And thus man tests his strength, his might, his inclination to become a man-god. Man becomes possessed by some "idea" and in this state his freedom begins to disappear; he becomes the slave of some outside force. Dostoevsky depicted this process with unexampled power. He who in his self-will knows no limits to his freedom, loses his freedom, gradually is possessed by an "idea" that enslaves him. Such a one is Raskolnikov. He in no way gives the impression of a free man. He is a maniac possessed by a false "idea." He has no moral independence, because moral independence comes through self-purification and self-liberation. What is the nature of Raskolnikov's "idea"? Everybody in Dostoevsky has his "idea." Raskolnikov tests the limits of his own nature, of human nature in general. He believes that he belongs to the elect of humanity—not to the ordinary people, but to the extraordinary people who are called upon to be the benefactors of humanity. He thinks that everything is possible and wants to test his powers. And thus Dostoevsky reduces the moral task confronting a man with such a consciousness to an elementary theorem. This extraordinary man who feels called upon to serve humanity: has he the right to kill even the meanest and ugliest human creature, a disgusting old woman and pawnbroker who brings nothing but evil to human beings, in order thus to open a way for himself into the future, a future where he can do good for mankind? Is this permissible? Now in *Crime and Punishment* Dostoevsky shows with striking power that this is not permissible, that such a man spiritually murders himself. Here is an experiment that is experienced immanently. Dostoevsky shows that all is not permissible, because human nature is created in the image and likeness of God, and therefore every man has an absolute value. The spiritual nature of man will not sanction the self-willed murder of even the lowest and most harmful of people. When man in his self-will destroys another man, he destroys himself as well, ceases to be a man, loses his human image, and his personality begins to disintegrate. No "idea," no "lofty" goal can justify a criminal attitude to even the lowest of one's neighbors. A "neighbor" is more precious than some "distant" being; every human life, every human soul is worth more than this philanthropy directed toward future mankind, than abstract "ideas." Such is Christian consciousness. And Dostoevsky reveals it. Raskolnikov imagined himself Napoleon, a great man, a man-god; this man, after stepping over those limits established by human-nature-in-the-likeness-of-God, falls precipitously, learns that he is not a superman but a helpless, abject, trembling creature. Raskolnikov recognizes his absolute helplessness, his nothingness. The testing of the limits of his freedom and of his might had disastrous results. Along with a worthless, harmful old lady, Raskolnikov destroyed himself. After the "crime," which was pure experiment, he lost his freedom and was crushed by his impotence. He no longer had left even a proud consciousness. He learned that it is easy to kill a man, that this experiment is not so difficult, but that strength is not obtained from it; rather it deprives man of spiritual strength. Nothing "great," "extraordinary," world-shaking in significance occurred because Raskolnikov killed the pawnbroker: he was crushed by the emptiness of all that occurred. The eternal law asserted its rights and he submitted to its authority. Christ came not to violate but to fulfill the law. And the freedom which the New Testament brings with it does not rebel against the Old Testament, but only opens up a more lofty world. And Raskolnikov inevitably had to succumb to the force of immutable Old Testament law. The truly great, the men of genius who did great things for all of mankind, did not act in the manner of Raskolnikov. They did not consider themselves supermen to whom everything was permitted; they unselfishly served that which they put above man, and for this very reason were able to give so much to mankind. Raskolnikov is above all a divided man of reflexion; his freedom, to begin with, is voided by an inner disease. The genuinely great men were not in that state: they were marked by wholeness. Dostoevsky exposes the falseness of all pretensions to being a superman. He shows that the false notion of the superman ruins man, that pretension to unlimited strength betrays weakness and importance. All these contemporary strivings toward superhuman might are paltry and pitiful; they end with man toppling into inhuman weakness. And moral and religious conscience proves in its essence to be eternal. The pangs of conscience not only expose crime, but also expose the impotence of man in his false pretensions to might. Raskolnikov's pangs of conscience reveal not only that he stepped over the limits of the permissible, but they also expose weakness and paltriness.

The theme of Raskolnikov signifies in the final analysis the crisis of humanism, the end of humanistic morality, the disaster of man that follows on self-assertion. The appearance of the dream of the superman and of the notion of the superman and a higher human morality, signifies that humanism is over and done with, defunct. There is no humanitarianism left in Raskolnikov, his attitude toward his neighbor is cruel and merciless. Man, a living, suffering, concrete human being must be sacrificed upon the altar of the superhuman "idea." In the name of some "distant" being, some "distant" abstraction, one can act any way one pleases with one's "neighbor," with man. Dostoevsky himself preaches the religion of love for one's "neighbor" and he exposes the lies of a religion of love for the "distant" one, the abstract and superhuman. There is a "distant" one who preached love for one's "neighbor." That one was God. But the idea of God is the only superhuman idea which does not destroy man, does not transform man into a mere means and tool. God reveals himself through His Son. And His Son is the perfect God and the perfect man, the God-Man in whom the divine and the human are perfectly united. Every other superhuman idea annihilates man, transforms him into a means, a tool. The idea of the man-god bears with it death to man. This truth may be seen in the example of Nietzsche. Equally fatal for mankind is Marx's idea of the inhuman collective, in the religion of socialism. Dostoevsky studies in its various forms, individual and mass, the fatal consequences that come when man is possessed by the idea of the man-god. Here the kingdom of the human comes to an end and there is not even mercy for man. Humaneness was the reflection of the Christian truth about man. The final betrayal of this truth abrogates humane respect for man. In the name of the grandeur of the superman, in the name of the happiness of a distant, future mankind, in the name of world revolution, in the name of the boundless freedom of the one or the boundless equality of all, it becomes permissible to torture or put to death any man, any number of people, to turn any person into a mere tool for a great "idea," a great goal. Everything is permitted in the name of the boundless freedom of the superman (extreme individualism) or in the name of the boundless equality of mankind (extreme collectivism). Human self-will is given the right to determine as it sees fit the value of human life and the right to dispose of it at will. In this view, human life is not God's, nor is His the last judgment. Man, puffed up with himself as the possessor of the superhuman "idea," assumes these rights. And his judgment is merciless, godless and inhuman. Dostoevsky exhaustively explores in their individual and collective forms the fateful manifestations of human self-will; he unmasks the enticing lie. Raskolnikov is one of those possessed by that kind of false idea. He himself, in his self-will and lawlessness, decides whether one can kill even the most unregenerate of men in the name of his "idea." Yet it is not for man, but for God to resolve this question. God is the only higher "idea," and he who does not bow before the Higher Will in resolving this question annihilates his neighbor and himself. The meaning of *Crime and Punishment* rests in this truth.

The Problem of Guilt

by Alfred L. Bem

It is often said that Dostoevsky's "novel-tragedy" gravitates toward a single major "catastrophic" event, one usually connected with a crime; what has not been sufficiently stressed is that Dostoevsky's focus is not crime at all, but its corollary—guilt. . . . We shall not be concerned here with any objective norms of guilt and crime, but only with those psychological substrata on which these norms rest. . . . Crime will be understood only as the *awareness by the subject himself of some moral norm which he has violated,* quite apart from whether this violation has been recognized externally, morally, as a real crime. Without such a limitation [in the definition of crime] the correlation between guilt and crime, which plays such a crucial role in Dostoevsky, would be incomprehensible. Quite often, particularly in Dostoevsky's earlier works,[1] the feeling of guilt becomes extremely and even tragically intense when only an extremely vague sense of a concrete crime lends support to this feeling. In other words, the objective crime which awakens a feeling of guilt may turn out to be so insignificant as to provide no explanation for the intense feeling of guilt. In this case the tragedy of guilt can be understood and disclosed only by presupposing that the *concrete crime serves as a surrogate for some crime not openly manifested yet present in the psyche,* like a trauma or pressure of conscience.

To understand Dostoevsky's thought one must allow for the presence in the human psyche of a feeling of sinfulness as such, independent of the existence of any concrete crime—what we might call *the feeling of original sin.* . . . We can assume, then, that the feeling of sin, of guilt can be present in the psyche unaccompanied by any consciousness of crime. Indeed, the guilt-ridden consciousness often seeks a crime, as though it wished to free itself from an overwhelming sense of fatality and enter the world of ordinary human criminality, apparently more tolerable to human consciousness than the intense pressure of metaphysical sinfulness. It is only here that we can find an explanation for Dos-

From "Problemy viny" ["*The Problem of Guilt"*] *in* Dostoevskij, *by Alfred L. Bem (Berlin, 1938), 142–148; 167–168. Translated from the Russian by Robert Louis Jackson.*
[1] Bem's analysis of the problem of guilt in Dostoevsky's early works is omitted from this translation. [ED.]

toevsky's idea that "each of us is guilty for all," and for his characteristic notion of the "desire to suffer." With the latter in mind we can turn to the episode in *Crime and Punishment* with the house painter Mikolka, the workman who takes on himself Raskolnikov's crime. The episode is a minor one, but of central importance for our theme.

No one first meeting the painter Mikolka Dementiev suspected in him a spiritual complexity which would lead to his puzzling assumption of guilt for the murder of the old lady. We find an ingenuous, life-loving lad, with a taste for the bottle. Porfiry Petrovich, a man not without insight, characterizes him this way:

> First he's immature, still a child; and not that he's a coward, but sensitive, a kind of artist type. Yes, really. You mustn't laugh at me for explaining him like that. He is innocent and completely impressionable. He has feelings; he is a fantast. He can sing and dance, and they say he can tell stories so people gather from all around to listen. And he'll go to school and he'll laugh himself silly because somebody somehow crooked a finger at him; and he'll drink himself senseless, not because he's a drunkard, but just every now and then, when people buy him drinks; he's like a child still. (VI, 2)

This characterization tallies completely with our first impression of the house painters on the day of the murder. The witnesses unanimously testified that there was nothing suspicious in their conduct. Both painters, Nikolai and Dmitri, ran out of the courtyard and began to pummel each other in fun. . . . How is it possible that this apparently simple person could come to take on himself somebody else's crime? This psychological enigma must be solved, and Dostoevsky does so; but as usual when a psychological explanation is to be found in the unconscious, Dostoevsky provides an explanation on a conscious level: in this case, introducing the motif of "fear" that he, Mikolka, would be convicted. This fear overcomes Mikolka when he learns about the murder of the old lady and feels guilty because he had picked up the earrings dropped by the murderer; his fear of being accused became unbearable and he wants to hang himself. Dostoevsky tries to give the reader a convincing explanation of Mikolka's behavior by making us aware of Mikolka's internal distress; but he does not yet make it clear to us why Mikolka decided to assume somebody else's guilt. Porfiry Petrovich hints at the reason for this strange behavior; he suggests that the explanation must be sought elsewhere in Mikolka's moral experiences. The house painter turns out not to be so spiritually uncomplicated as we had imagined; he has his own enigmatic past. Porfiry Petrovich observes:

> But did you know that he was a Raskolnik [schismatic, sectarian—ED.]? Well, not a Raskolnik, exactly, but a member of one of those religious sects. There were members of his family who were Runners; they'd run away from wordly involvement. He himself actually spent two years, not long ago, under the spiritual tutelage of some holy elder in some village . . . He himself was moved to run off into the wilderness! He had the

spirit, would pray to God at night, read the old "true" books and reread them, for hours on end. . . . Well, now, in jail it seems he remembered the honorable elder, and the Bible turned up again, too. Do you know what they mean, Rodion Romanych, when they talk of "taking suffering upon themselves"? They don't mean suffering for anybody in particular, just "one has to suffer." That means, *accept* suffering; and if it's from the authorities, so much the better. . . . You mean you won't admit that our people produce fantastic characters of this sort? Yes, many. Now the elder is beginning to have some effect again, especially after that business with the noose. (VI, 2)

The way was clearly prepared for Mikolka's "fantastic" behavior. The news of the murder which had so disconcerted him and led him to attempt suicide was only the most immediate cause which brought to the surface those feelings of guilt that were hidden in the depths of his unconscious.

Precisely the problem of guilt lay at the root of Mikolka's act, not a superficial "fear" of conviction; indeed, Dostoevsky originally had no intention at all of introducing the latter motive. Twice in the notebooks to the novel he stresses the basic "religious" motive in Mikolka's behavior. Thus, in one part of the manuscript we read: "A workman testifies against himself (he had got caught up with religion), wanted to suffer (but gets muddled). They start pressuring him. And an old man sits there: one has to suffer, he says." A brief note appears in another place. "News at the gathering that a man (a workman) was taken by religion."

We can see from these notes that the root of Mikolka's behavior lay in a "religious" feeling linked with his moral experiences. The fact that Dostoevsky associates these elements in Mikolka's consciousness with the influence of some old religious sectarian serving a prison term with him testifies to Dostoevsky's artistic awareness. Such views on the primordial sinfulness of man were widespread in Russian sectarian religious thought.

One might suspect Dostoevsky of using the whole Mikolka episode only as an artful manoeuvre in the development of a detective story, a way of mixing the cards and holding back the denouement. But his supreme artistry is revealed in another way: concerned with narrative technique, he nevertheless introduces instead of a shallow plot device an incident which is closely connected with the central idea of the novel—the problem of guilt. The house painter, in contradistinction to Raskolnikov who strives to evade responsibility before his conscience for his sin, assumes responsibility for a crime that he did not commit. The interplay between these two responses to the problem of guilt will become even clearer after we examine Raskolnikov's crime.

Mikolka, according to Dostoevsky, "got caught up with religion" under the influence of an old religious sectarian; but in order to get caught up on religion he must have had some spiritual motivation. We must therefore assume a feeling of general sinfulness, of primordial guilt in the

depths of Mikolka's consciousness, or, more accurately, in his unconscious
—a feeling which sought expression in taking suffering upon himself. The
"desire to suffer" cannot be explained without the supposition that there
is a primordial feeling of guilt, the experience of primordial sinfulness,
at the basis of the human soul. The incident involving Mikolka in *Crime
and Punishment* is only an artistic expression of this phenomenon observed by Dostoevsky in the depths of his own being. . . .

Raskolnikov, a prisoner of his *idée fixe,* kills an old money lender. The
whole novel is built around the unique process of disintegration in the
hero's soul: his intellectual life is split off from the life of feeling. I do
not know how I can express my thought more precisely here. A state of
spiritual unity and harmony gives way to a "disintegration" in which one
aspect of a person's being becomes overextended and eclipses the rest.
But though driven into the unconscious these other aspects of self can
remain active there and affect conduct in a special way. It is still possible
then, paradoxically, for a criminal in his acts to preserve some inner nobility: just this inner split in Raskolnikov is the content of *Crime and
Punishment.*

Crime is presented here as an unquestioned fact, not only in the formal
but also the moral sense. But this fact does not penetrate Raskolnikov's
consciousness; it takes the form in his unconscious of a potential power
of conscience. To the very end, mind remains unrepentant. Even in
prison, after his conviction, Raskolnikov still holds inflexibly to the idea
that the murder is justifiable. And yet his whole being, his entire moral
nature is shaken precisely by the moral aspect of the murder. Like a
shadow, Sonia continually follows him and directs him onto the path of
repentance. Dostoevsky portrays this symbolic role of Sonia with amazing
power. When Raskolnikov wavers in his decision to confess, Sonia at that
very moment is with him as his embodied conscience. As he leaves the
police station he sees her:

> There, not far from the gate, stood Sonia, numb and deathly pale; and
> she looked at him with a wild look. He stopped before her. There was
> something painful and tortured in her face, something desperate. She
> threw up her hands. A ghastly, lost smile forced its way to his lips. He
> stood there and grinned. Then he turned back upstairs to the station.
> (VI, 8)

His fate is decided: he confesses to killing the old woman.

Here, then, is an extraordinary situation: in the absence of any conscious guilt feeling, guilt is not only subconsciously present but even de-
termines the final outcome of the spiritual drama. Thus, Dostoevsky is
right when he envisages the possibility, too, of Raskolnikov's spiritual
resurrection, that is, the restoration of his spiritual unity.

The World of Raskolnikov

by Joseph Frank

Most Western criticism of Dostoevsky, when it is not searching his work for religious sustenance, approaches him from a psychological or biographical point of view. The overwhelming and immediate impression made by Dostoevsky's works on first reading is that of a passionate exploration of abnormal states of divided consciousness; and it has been only natural to assume that so masterly a portrayal of internal psychological conflict could only come from direct experience. Hence Dostoevsky's biography has been endlessly explored, analysed, and speculated about in the hope of uncovering some traumatic key to his creations.

Russian criticism since the Bolshevik Revolution has, of course, taken a different tack. It has tried to interpret him either in socio-psychological terms (he is a member of the "dispossessed and rootless petty-bourgeois intelligentsia," whose characters reflect all the abnormalities of this class), or it has engaged in genuine historical investigation and turned up numerous interesting relations between Dostoevsky's novels and the cultural history of his time. (In fairness, I should also mention the excellent stylistic researches of such critics as Leonid Grossman, Yuri Tynyanov, and V. V. Vinogradov, which form the basis for our contemporary understanding of Dostoevsky's art.) Since Dostoevsky, however, is still the most brilliant and devastating opponent of the men who provide the foundations for present Soviet culture—not Marx and Engels, but the Russian radical tradition of Belinsky and Chernyshevsky—Soviet historical study of Dostoevsky is inevitably handicapped in scope and myopic in interpretation.

Without accepting the theoretical premises of the Soviet approach to Dostoevsky, I believe, nonetheless, that the Russians are right in stressing the social and cultural dimensions of his work. For the exclusive Western emphasis on psychology and personal biography as a means of access to Dostoevsky's mind and art is unquestionably very limiting and very falsifying. I should probably argue the same in the case of any writer; but since my subject at the moment is not critical method, I shall only say

"The World of Raskolnikov," by Joseph Frank. From Encounter 26, no. 6 *(June, 1966): 30–35. Copyright © 1966 by Encounter Ltd. Reprinted by permission of the publisher and author.*

that, of all the great modern writers, this type of biographical criticism seems to me *least* illuminating as regards Dostoevsky.

If Dostoevsky has one claim to fame, it is certainly as a great *ideological* novelist—perhaps not the greatest, for that would involve comparisons with Sterne and Cervantes, but at least the greatest in the 19th century. And if his status as such is so generally accepted, it must be because his creative imagination was stimulated primarily by the problems of his society and his time rather than by his personal problems and private dilemmas. Or, to put the point the other way round, he was always able to project these private dilemmas in terms that linked up with the sharp conflict of attitudes and values occurring in the Russia of his time.

This is the reason why psychology in Dostoevsky's novels, vivid and unforgettable though it may be, is invariably only an instrument or tool used for a thematic purpose that is ultimately moral-ethical and ideological in import—ideological in the sense that all moral values are connected in Dostoevsky's sensibility with the future destiny of Russian life and culture. More particularly, he saw all moral and ethical issues in the light of the inner psychological problems posed for the Russian intelligentsia by the necessity of assimilating (and living by) alien Western European ideas. Dostoevsky's extensive journalism of the early 1860s (most of which has not yet been translated) or, more accessibly, his travel-articles about Europe, *Winter Notes on Summer Impressions* (1863), contain a whole history of Russian culture conceived in terms of this inner struggle. We cannot take even the first step towards understanding his major aim as a novelist, if we do not realise that he wished to portray the *new* types and modalities of this perennial Russian inner struggle springing up all around him in the turbulent and evolving Russia of the 1860s and 1870s.

It is from this point of view that we must take very seriously Dostoevsky's claim to "realism" for his novels—a claim which, in my opinion, is entirely justified. But let us be clear about the nature of this "realism" and the nature of Dostoevsky's imagination. He knew very well that he was not a "realist" in the sense of getting the normal, middle range of private and social experience on the page. This was why he spoke of his bent for "fantastic realism"; but what he meant by this term was something very clear and very specific. He meant that the process of his creation would invariably start from some doctrine that he found prevalent among the Russian radical intelligentsia. It was there in black-and-white in the magazines or novels everybody was reading, and in this sense was perfectly "real"—particularly since Dostoevsky believed in the reality of ideas. But then he would take this doctrine and imagine its most extreme consequences *if* it were really to be put into practice and carried through in all its implications; and this was where his psychological gifts came in to aid him in dramatising the "fantasy" of this idea relentlessly translated into life.

Dostoevsky was perfectly well aware that the extremism he depicted in such a character as Raskolnikov was not at all the way in which the vast majority of the radical intelligentsia would hold the doctrines in question, or the way in which it would affect their lives. But then, the people who accepted the theories of Leibnitz in the 18th century bore little resemblance in real life to Dr. Pangloss and his pupil Candide. Nonetheless, we cannot deny that *Candide* dramatises a "real" fact of 18th-century culture. (It is suggestive that among the unfinished projects that Dostoevsky left at the time of his death was that of writing a Russian *Candide*.) Exactly the same relation obtains between the theories of Dostoevsky's protagonists, the acts to which their theories drive them, and the Russian culture of their time. Indeed, I think the best way to define Dostoevsky's particular uniqueness as a novelist is to call him a writer whose imagination naturally inclined to the *conte philosophique*, but who, happening to be born in the century of the realistic novel, possessed enough psychological genius to give his characters verisimilitude and to fuse one *genre* with the other. This, by the way, is one reason for the often-noted resemblance between *Notes from Underground* and *Le neveu de Rameau,* aside from the fact that 18th-century mechanical materialism was as important in the Russia of the 1860s as it had been in the France of Diderot.

I should now like to apply this general view of Dostoevsky to some of the problems involved in the interpretation of his first great novel, *Crime and Punishment.* If Dostoevsky invariably began with some doctrine of the Russian radical intelligentsia, what was his starting-point in this case? An answer to this question will, I believe, not only provide an entry into the book, but also explain why *Crime and Punishment* emerged when it did in Dostoevsky's development. Ordinarily, this novel is linked with his prison-term in Siberia, first because of his use of this setting in the Epilogue, and secondly because this period was supposed to have focused his attention on the problem of crime and the psychology of the criminal. None of this needs to be denied; but if this were the whole story, it is impossible not to wonder why Dostoevsky did not write *Crime and Punishment* when he came out of imprisonment and wrote so many other things instead. The truth is that the novel as we know it could not have been conceived before 1865 because the situation of Russian culture that Dostoevsky could imagine as Raskolnikov had not existed before that time.

If we look at Russian culture in the early and mid-1860s—and this means, for our purposes, the doctrines of the radical intelligentsia—we can easily spot the "reality" that is incarnated in Raskolnikov. In the first place, all the radical intelligentsia were convinced that the theories of English Utilitarianism solved all the problems of ethics and personal conduct. This has caused a great deal of confusion because only in Russia do we find this peculiar blend of French Utopian Socialism, with its belief in the possibility of a future world of love and moral perfection, held conjointly with a view of human nature stemming from the egoistic individualism of Bentham and Mill. Even more, the Russian radicals believed in the doctrine of what they called "rational egoism" with their usual passionate extremism and fanaticism. To find anything similar to their belief in abstract reason as an infallible guide to the complexities of the moral life, we should have to go back to William Godwin. And I bring in Godwin's name here both because he had a direct influence in Russia through N. G. Chernyshevsky, the intellectual mentor of the radicals in the early 1860s, and also because the Russian cultural situation at this time closely parallels that of England in the period of the French Revolution.

Like Godwin, the Russians also strove to develop an ethics which—in the graphic words of Hazlitt's *The Spirit of the Age*—tried "to pass the Arctic Circle and Frozen Regions, where the understanding is no longer warmed by the affections. . . ." And no better commentary has ever been written on *Crime and Punishment* than the passage in *The Prelude* where Wordsworth explains how abstract reason dupes itself in its dialectic with the irrational:

> *This was the time, when, all things tending fast*
> *To depravation, speculative schemes—*
> *That promised to abstract the hopes of Man*
> *Out of his feelings, to be fixed thenceforth*
> *For ever in a purer element—*
> *Found ready welcome. Tempting region that*
> *For Zeal to enter and refresh herself,*
> *Where passions had the privilege to work,*
> *And never hear the sound of their own names.*

The last two lines of this passage define the theme of *Crime and Punishment* with far more exactitude than the mountain of critical literature on Dostoevsky. Indeed, if we are to understand the position of Dostoevsky and his intellectual allies (Apollon Grigoriev and Nikolai Strakhov) as they confronted the Russian radicals of the 1860s, we can do no better than to take as a guide the reaction of the first generation of English Romantics to the French Revolution. Moreover, if Godwin stimulated the radicals, then the works of Carlyle, who was an especial favourite of Apollon Grigoriev, furnished sustenance for the anti-radical camp.

Thus it is by no means accidental that we find Raskolnikov's crime planned on the basis of a Utilitarian calculus; this was the very essence of the matter for Dostoevsky. And we see too that, exactly like Godwin, Raskolnikov believes that his reason can overcome the most fundamental and deeply rooted human feelings. Godwin argued, it will be recalled, that reason would (or should) persuade him to leave his mother or sister burning in a fire and rescue Fénelon instead because, as he writes in *Political Justice,* "the illustrious Bishop of Cambrai was of more worth" to humanity. Whatever a Freudian might think of this argument, Godwin believed that it followed with impeccable logic from a Utilitarian calculus taking as its ultimate standard the universal good of humanity. Raskolnikov's conviction that he would be able to commit a perfect crime is based, we should notice, on exactly the same type of reasoning.

Ordinary criminals, Raskolnikov had theorised, rob and steal out of need or viciousness; and they break down at the moment of the crime, leaving all sorts of clues scattered about, because they inwardly accept the justice and validity of the law they are breaking. The irrational forces of their conscience interfere with the rational lucidity of their action. But, he was convinced, nothing of the kind would happen to him because he knew that his so-called crime was not a crime. Reason had persuaded him that the amount of harm his crime would do was far out-weighed by the amount of good it would allow him to accomplish. Hence his irrational conscience would not trouble and distort his reason, and he would not lose control of his nerves and make blunders.

This is one way in which the very conception of Raskolnikov springs from the ideology of the Russian radicals in the mid-1860s, and shapes the basic psychological conflict in the book between reason and the irrational. But another essential ideological component is derived from the evolution of Russian left-wing ideas between 1860 and 1865. In this period, for various reasons, we find a shift from the ideals of Utopian Socialism, with its semi-religious glorification of the people, to that of an embittered élitism, which stressed the right of a superior individual to act independently for the welfare of humanity.

The most important event in Russian culture between 1863 and 1865 was a public quarrel between two groups of radicals—the old Utopian Socialists, and the new Nihilists. Dostoevsky's magazine *Epoch* printed a number of articles analysing and commenting on this momentous dispute, and immediately recognised, with great perspicacity, that it marked a fateful moment in the evolution of radical ideas. "The sons have taken up arms against the fathers, one generation replaces another," ironically wrote Strakhov, then the chief critic of *Epoch*; "a thick journal, once progressive, has turned out to be backward, and in its place stands another thick journal, which has succeeded in going farther along the path of progress." Even more relevant is that Dostoevsky himself wrote an article about this internecine warfare between the radicals called "Schism (*Raskol*) Among the Nihilists"; and this is what the whole episode is still called in histories of Russian culture. All this was just a few months before Dostoevsky, after the collapse of *Epoch*, sketched out in a letter his idea for a story about a murder committed by a young student acting under the influence of certain "strange, incomplete ideas"; and we can, I think, relate this schism among the Nihilists to *Crime and Punishment* in two ways.

One is in the difference that Dostoevsky draws between the comic and harmless Utopian Socialist in the novel, Lebezyatnikov, and Raskolnikov himself, who is no longer a Utopian Socialist but a true Nihilist. The Utopian Socialist is in favour of peaceful propaganda, conversion to the cause by reason and persuasion (which is why he lends books to Sonia), and he believes that the salvation of humanity hinges on communal living arrangements. These matters had still been important just two years before, in the period of *Notes from Underground*; but things in Russia moved very fast, and it was now out-of-date. Raskolnikov looks on all this as ineffectual nonsense; he feels that time is running out, that it is necessary to act now and not be content with Utopian dreams of the future, and that the superior individual has the right and the obligation to strike a decisive blow by himself.

A second reflection of this new situation may be found in Raskolnikov's famous article "On Crime." For every idea in this text, it would be possible to supply a parallel quotation from *The Russian Word*, the "thick journal" that had become the Nihilist organ. The main spokesman for the Nihilists was Dimitri Pisarev, best known for his attacks on art as being useless—which is, of course, merely another application of the Utilitarian calculus. And if we go back and read Pisarev and his group, we find these undeniably genuine left-wing radicals exhibiting the utmost contempt for the people on whose behalf they presumably wish to change the world. We also find them using the arguments of Social Darwinism to establish the justice of the ineradicable distinction between the weak and the strong, and the *right* of the strong to trample on the weak and unworthy.

Indeed, one of the most pugnacious contributors to *The Russian Word*, Bartholomew Zaitsev, who later in exile became a follower of Bakunin, even defended Negro slavery on the ground that Negroes were biologically inferior and would otherwise be wiped out entirely in their struggle for life against the White race. This opinion was repudiated by the majority of the radicals, although Pisarev defended Zaitsev's premises if not his conclusions. Even though a minority opinion, however, this was exactly the sort of *consistent* application of Utilitarianism-cum-Nihilism that Dostoevsky believed revealed the true moral consequences of the new radical ideology. This context explains the "Nietzschean" aspects of Raskolnikov, which have been so often commented upon. Thomas Masaryk noted some of these "Nietzschean" elements in Pisarev and Russian Nihilism as far back as 1913, in his indispensable book *The Spirit of Russia*; but nobody has paid the slightest attention to them since, or brought them into any relation with Dostoevsky.

All this, I hope, has now placed us in a better position to understand what Dostoevsky was trying to do in *Crime and Punishment*. His aim, in my view, was to portray the inescapable contradictions in this radical ideology of Russian Nihilism. To do so, he adopted his usual procedure (in his mature work) of imagining its "strange, incomplete ideas" put into practice by an idealistic young man whose character traits embody its various conflicting aspects. Now Dostoevsky knew very well that the emotional impulses inspiring the average Russian radical were generous and self-sacrificing. They were moved by love, sympathy, altruism, the desire to aid, heal and comfort suffering—whatever they might believe about the hard-headedness of their "rational egoism." The underlying foundation of their moral nature was Christian and Russian (for Dostoevsky the two were the same), and in total disharmony with the superimposed Western ideas they had assimilated, and on whose basis they believed they were acting. Hence over and over again in Dostoevsky's major works we find him dramatising the inner conflict of a member of the Russian intelligentsia torn between his innate feelings and his conscious ideas, between the irrational (which, by the way, is never Freudian in Dostoevsky but always moral as in Shakespeare) and the amorality of reason in one form or another.

In *Crime and Punishment*, Dostoevsky set himself the task of portraying this conflict in the form of a self-awakening, the gradual discovery by Raskolnikov *himself* of the unholy mixture of incompatibles in his ideology. This is why Raskolnikov seems to have one motive for his crime at the beginning of the book and another towards the end, when he makes his famous confession to Sonia. Many critics have pointed to this seeming duality of motive as a weakness in the novel, and artistic failure on Dostoevsky's part to project his character unifiedly. On the other hand, Philip Rahv quite recently has maintained that this is precisely what makes the book great—that in failing to provide a clear and single motive Dostoevsky reveals "the problematical nature of the modern personality," or the startling fact "that human consciousness is inexhaustible and incalculable."

Both these views, however, are equally and egregiously wrong.[1] The whole point of the book lies precisely in the process by which Raskolnikov moves from one explanation of the crime to another, and in so doing discovers the truth about the nature of the deed he committed. Even without the historical background I have sketched in, this should be abundantly clear to anyone who has some respect for Dostoevsky's capacity as a craftsman, and who studies the curious and original construction of the first part of the novel.

[1] Philip Rahv's useful essay, "Dostoevsky in *Crime and Punishment*," has been widely reprinted and widely read since its original appearance in *Partisan Review* in 1960. It therefore seems advisable to correct an important error of fact that Mr. Rahv's essay has no doubt had the effect of propagating.

Mr. Rahv believes that he has discovered a long-overlooked "source" for Raskolnikov's theory of "the great man" in Hegel's *Philosophy of History*. As evidence of Dostoevsky's acquaintance with this text, he cites a letter of Dostoevsky's (22 February 1854) in which, among a list of other books requested, Dostoevsky says "be sure to send Hegel, particularly Hegel's *Philosophy of History*. . . ." A comparison with the original, however, reveals that Dostoevsky asked for Hegel's *History of Philosophy* and not the *Philosophy of History*.

Why, for example, does Dostoevsky begin his narrative just a day before the actual commission of the crime, and convey Raskolnikov's *conscious* motivation in a series of flashbacks? One reason, of course, is to
obtain the brilliant effect of dramatic irony at the close of Part I. For the
entire process of reasoning that leads to Raskolnikov's theory of the altruistic Utilitarian crime is only explained in detail in the tavern-scene,
where Raskolnikov hears his very own theory discussed by another student and a young officer; and this scene is the last important one just before the crime is committed. (It may be well, incidentally, to recall that
when the officer doubts the possibility of anyone committing such a crime,
the student retorts that, if this were so, "there would never have been a
single great man." The "great man" component of Raskolnikov's theory
is thus there from the very first, and is not unexpectedly tacked on later.)
Temporally, the tavern-scene and the murder itself are at the very opposite ends of a single time-sequence; but they are telescoped together deftly
by Dostoevsky's narrative technique—and for a very important purpose.
And if we grasp the thematic significance of Dostoevsky's dramatic irony
here, I think it will give us a model to illuminate the whole vexed question of Raskolnikov's motivation.

The purpose of Dostoevsky's juxtaposition and telescoping of the time-
sequence is obviously to undermine Raskolnikov's *conscious* motivation
for the reader. The hypnotic hysteria in which he kills the old pawnbroker could not reveal more clearly, in an objective, dramatic fashion,
that Raskolnikov's crime is not being committed according to his altruistic, Utilitarian theory. Whatever Raskolnikov may have believed about
himself, he is now acting in the grip of other forces and not on the basis
of the theory, which is still fresh in our minds because we have met it
only a page or two before. Dostoevsky's technique is thus intended to
force the reader, if he is at all attentive, to pose to himself the question
of what Raskolnikov's *true* motive can possibly be.

Now I believe that the entire construction of the first part of the book
is intended to give an answer to this question in the same objective, dramatic fashion. Part I consists of two alternating sequences of episodes. In
one sequence, composed largely of flashbacks, we learn about Raskolnikov's past, his desperate family situation, and all the circumstances push-
ing him towards the crime. All these scenes build up the altruistic side of
his character, and reinforce our sense of his essential goodness, humanity,
and sympathy for suffering. It is this aspect of his nature which forever
distinguishes him from a real criminal, and that makes him think of ex-
piating his crime—if one can really call it a crime—by future services to
humanity. But then we also see him in *action* in this part, in the series of
episodes with Marmeladov and his family, and with the young girl on the
boulevard. And in these scenes we notice a very significant dialectic occurring, which undermines the foundations of his altruistic, Utilitarian

theory in exactly the same way as the later dramatic irony; this latter is, indeed, only the final crescendo of this whole masterly sequence.

In each of these episodes, Raskolnikov at first responds purely instinctively to the spectacle of human misery and suffering, and he spontaneously rushes to help and to succour. But at a certain point, a total transformation of his personality occurs from one moment to the next. Suddenly he withdraws, becomes indifferent and contemptuous, and instead of pitying mankind he begins to hate it for being weak and contemptible. In each case, this change of feeling is indicated to be the result of the application of a Utilitarian calculus. For example, he is starving and yet leaves all his money at the Marmeladovs; but as he walks out he begins to laugh at himself scornfully for this gesture. Why? Because, he thinks, "after all they have Sonia and I need it myself." This leads him into reflections on how despicable human beings are because they can become accustomed to anything—like living off the income of a prostitute daughter.

The same situation occurs at greater length with the girl on the boulevard, who has clearly once already been violated and who is in danger of falling into the hands of another seducer. Raskolnikov at first springs to her aid, but then again turns away with a cold revulsion of feeling. "Let them eat themselves," he says to himself (after all, a good Darwinian sentiment). And then he ponders the Malthusian proposition that a "percentage" has to go that way anyhow for the protection of society, so that pity and sympathy are totally misplaced. The "percentage" theory has recently been traced in Russian scholarship to an article of Zaitsev's in *The Russian Word,* who used it for the philanthropic purpose of arguing that, since vice and crime were inevitable natural phenomena, it was wrong to punish their perpetrators. Dostoevsky's use of the same idea for Raskolnikov, however, is perhaps more logical in taking the greatest good of the greatest number as a standard.

Each step, then, in the *backward* process of revealing Raskolnikov's conscious, altruistic motive for the contemplated crime is accompanied by another episode moving *forward* in time that undercuts it, and that reveals the *true* effect of his ideas on his feelings. In each case the reader can see clearly that when Raskolnikov acts under the influence of his Utilitarian ideas, he unleashes in himself a cold and pitiless egomaniac who hates humanity although he continues to believe that he loves it. This repeated dramatic illustration of how Raskolnikov's ideas twist and distort his feelings may perhaps explain why even those critics who taxed Dostoevsky with inconsistency of motive have never gone so far as to claim that his supposed artistic lapse seriously damaged the novel. Clearly, these critics could feel the inner unity of Raskolnikov, even though, on the basis of their misreading of the book, it was impossible for them to explain what this unity was or how it was obtained.

I have perhaps said enough now to explain why it is really no surprise when Raskolnikov confesses to Sonia that he had committed the crime for himself alone, and solely to see whether he was strong enough to have the right to kill. This is merely his own self-recognition of what Dostoevsky has been making the reader feel ever since the first pages of the book. Let me conclude, however, with a few more observations on Dostoevsky's extremely skilful handling of the relation between structure and theme in *Crime and Punishment*.

In Part II, Dostoevsky begins to close the gap that exists between the reader's awareness of Raskolnikov and Raskolnikov's awareness of himself. For in Part II, as he begins to recover from his illness, Raskolnikov starts to ponder all the anomalies of the crime and to realise that he no longer knows *why* it was committed. At this point he is confronted with his old article "On Crime," which reveals to what extent egomania had always been an inseparable part of the Utilitarian love of humanity. Dostoevsky withholds the full development of this motif, though he had carefully foreshadowed it earlier, until it becomes relevant both to answer Raskolnikov's own questions about his crime and to crystallise and define the reader's earlier impressions. The experience of the crime, however, has now shown Raskolnikov that the feelings which inspired his altruistic love of humanity cannot co-exist in the same sensibility with those necessary to be a Napoleon, a Solon, or a Lycurgus. For the true great man, possessed by his sense of mission, cannot have any thoughts to spare for the suffering humanity on whom he tramples for their own future happiness.

 Once Raskolnikov's original theory breaks apart in this way, he is then confronted with the choice between non-Utilitarian Christian love and self-sacrifice in Sonia or total amorality leading to self-destruction in Svidrigailov. The construction of the latter half of the book thus clearly reflects its purpose, which was to persuade Dostoevsky's readers among the radical intelligentsia that they had to choose between a doctrine of love and a doctrine of power. Both were embodied, as I have tried to show, in the strange mixture of impulses and ideas that went by the name of Russian Nihilism. And that Dostoevsky's attacks did have some effect may be indicated by the change that occurred in Russian radical ideology in the 1870s, when "rational egoism" was abandoned for a secularised Christian ethics of love.

As a footnote, let me add that I have always been intrigued by the information that the high-strung young Pisarev broke down and wept when he read *Crime and Punishment*. Was there any shock of recognition involved in this response? If so, it did not prevent him from immediately writing an article, which has since become a classic in Russian criticism, proving that Raskolnikov's crime was really caused by hunger and malnutrition.

Raskolnikov's Theory on the "Rights" of Great Men and Napoleon III's *History of Caesar*

by *F. I. Evnin*

Raskolnikov's theory . . . arose ultimately out of Russian life in the 1860s; but what undoubtedly helped crystallize Dostoevsky's thinking on the subject was an extensive discussion both in the West and in Russia, in February, March and April 1865 (several months before Dostoevsky went to work on the novel) on the question of the role and rights of "extraordinary people." The discussion turned on Napoleon III's *History of Caesar.*[1] This book, much heralded and widely advertised, was one of the great sensations of 1865. The book came on the market in Paris at the beginning of March and was immediately translated into almost all European languages. A Russian translation, preceded by big advertisements in the newspapers, appeared April 3. But the broad reading public had had advance information on the work of the newly born "historian": countless articles, surveys and reviews literally flooded the February and March issues of Russian newspapers and journals. Materials reproduced from the French, English and Belgian press also expressed the opinions of many Russian observers.

Here are some of the maxims on the role and significance of "extraordinary people" from the preface to the emperor's book:

> When extraordinary deeds attest to a superior genius, what could be more repellent to common sense than to attribute to this genius all the passions and all the thoughts of the average man? What could be more false than not to recognize the superiority of these exceptional beings who appear in history from time to time and, like bright beacons, scatter the gloom of their epoch and illuminate the future? Providence sends such people as

---

"Raskolnikov's Theory on the 'Rights' of Great Men and Napoleon III's History of Caesar" [Editor's title]. Excerpt from an essay, "Prestuplenie i nakazanie" ["Crime and Punishment"] by F. I. Evnin, in Tvorchestvo Dostoevskogo [Dostoevsky's Creative Work], *ed. N. Stepanov (Moscow, 1959), pp. 153–157. Translated from the Russian by Robert Louis Jackson.*

[1] Napoléon III (Charles-Louis-Napoléon Bonaparte, 1803–73), French politician and emperor, published *Histoire de César* (2 vols.) in 1865–66. [*ed.*]

Caesar, Karl the Great, Napoleon in order to chart for the peoples the course which they must follow, to put the mark of their genius on the new era and, in a few years, to complete the work of many centuries. Happy the peoples who comprehend and follow after them! Woe to those who do not recognize and who oppose them! They act like Jews, they crucify their Messiah; they are blind and criminal.

What is of central interest to us is not the book's content but . . . the mere fact that the question of "great men" had become an issue of broad public interest. . . .

Here are some excerpts from some European essays which attacked the Emperor's book. These essays were wholly or partly reproduced in Russian journals and newspapers. The notion that "heroes" are morally responsible for their conduct is the leitmotif of the journalist E. Forcade in the March 1865 number of *Revue des deux mondes*.

As for the morality of their acts, we have no doubt that it must be founded on that law of justice which is revealed in the conscience that is found in all men alike . . . But all this greatness that superior men derive from their own gifts and from the position they occupy is not sufficient justification for their career and their work. Before imposing on peoples a religious submission to the glorious instruments of historical necessity, one must look at the morality of their acts. . . .

The English observer of *The Morning Herald* emphasizes these same moral criteria: "The majority of our countrymen have always believed and always will, that all historical events and all the actions of people, great or small, contain truth and untruth, and that law must triumph at all times."

The French and English journalists are obviously concerned with the core of Raskolnikov's "theory": "the 'extraordinary' man has the right— I don't mean the official right; but he has the right to decide in his own conscience whether to transgress—certain obstacles." The progressive Russian press, of course, roundly condemned the efforts of the crowned "historian" to sanction freedom from all moral restraints. . . .

The emperor's book is extensively analyzed in *The Contemporary* (*Sovremennik*), No. 2, 1865, by one "W" in an article entitled "What is the Meaning of Great Men in History?" The core of the writer's critique of Napoleon III's views in the thesis that great men are the creations of their century and not its creators. And in a passage especially relevant to our theme, the writer ironically stresses the need to find ways to distinguish "great" men from "average" ones. These lines strikingly recall the words of Porfiry Petrovich in *Crime and Punishment* when he sarcastically discusses the same problem with Raskolnikov. In *The Contemporary* we read:

Thus, there are two different kinds of human logic, just as there are different moral laws. One brand of logic and set of laws by which one ought to judge the acts of ordinary people; another logic and other laws by which one ought to judge the world's geniuses, heroes and demigods . . . But if the great geniuses are spared ordinary laws, if the laws of ordinary logic do not apply to them, then the question arises: how shall we recognize such individuals? . . . I dare say we might judge one person to be a simple mortal, while he might turn out to be a genius; or suddenly we would take somebody for a genius, while he might turn out to be a quite average, run-of-the-mill type.

And in *Crime and Punishment* Porfiry Petrovich observes:

In this gentleman's article all people are divisible into "ordinary" and "extraordinary." The ordinary must live obediently and have no right to transgress the law—because, you see, they're ordinary. The extraordinary, on the other hand, have the right to commit all kinds of crimes and to transgress the law in all kinds of ways, for the simple reason that they are extraordinary . . . Tell me this, though. How do you go about telling the extraordinary ones from the ordinary? Are they marked from birth? I believe we need to be a little more accurate here, a somewhat more external distinction, so to speak. . . . Because you'll agree, if there should be any kind of mix-up and somebody from one part should imagine he belonged to the other part, and if he started "eliminating all obstacles," as you so felicitously put it, then there's a * * * (III, 5)

These excerpts, I think, speak for themselves. There seems little doubt that there is an organic link between the response of the progressive press to Napoleon III's book and the "idea" and image of Raskolnikov. . . . Dostoevsky criticized the theory of special "rights" of great men from a position quite different from that of *The Contemporary* in the article sign by "W." . . . Raskolnikov's "theory" has its roots in Russian reality of the 1860s and its social, ethical and philosophical aspects are undoubtedly its most important.[2] Nonetheless, its topical political frame of reference . . . the genetic link with a critique of Bonapartism, Caesarism, is not without interest . . . When he condemns the theory and action of his own "candidate for Napoleon," Dostoevsky himself sharply censures the ideology of Bonapartism, of blood and filth, which marked both the "great" Napoleon and the "little" Napoleon.

[2] Evnin also refers in his essay to a number of writings and fictional characters in the nineteenth century that in his view anticipate or recall aspects of Raskolnikov's "theory," e.g. *Das Einzige und sein Eigentum* [*The Ego and his Own*] (1845) by Max Stirner; the novel *Eugene Aram* (1835) by Edward Bulwer-Lytton, First Baron (1803–73); Balzac's heroes Vautrin, Rastignac, Lucien de Rubembré; Theodor Mommsen's *Römische Geschichte* [*History of Rome*] (1854–56); Tolstoy's *War and Peace* (1863–68). [ED.]

Toward Regeneration

by Yury F. Karyakin

In *Crime and Punishment*, after Porfiry finally "catches" Raskolnikov and he confesses to the murder, many readers and critics, losing interest in the novel, give the epilogue only a perfunctory reading. After all, they think, everything is clear without it: the crime has been exposed, punishment has followed. What more is necessary?

But the crime and punishment of which Dostoevsky wrote is something else again. He looked at the criminal and civil code from a philosophical point of view. He examined legal questions and even the "detective story" features of the novel in the context of his own world outlook. Without the epilogue we should have a distorted view of *Crime and Punishment;* it is not only a formal conclusion, but a necessary finale where the main knots are disentangled or sundered (though new ones, still to be loosened, are formed here too).

Only in the epilogue does Raskolnikov reap the ultimate consequences of his crime—there is nothing beyond: the death of his mother, his rejection even by the convict community and, in his nightmare, doomsday. *Crime and Punishment* is not only a novel about the murder of an old woman, a moneylender, but a novel about matricide, about the moral suicide of a criminal and about the potential self-destruction of humanity.

Only in the epilogue does Raskolnikov become convinced of the boundless love and faith of those close to him and ready to sacrifice themselves for him—his mother, Sonia, his sister, Razumikhin. *Crime and Punishment,* then, is a novel not only about the extremes of evil the criminal inflicts on others, but also about people's unlimited goodness, a goodness which can save the criminal.

Only in the epilogue does Raskolnikov recognize the full depths of his crime and find in himself forces to correct the wrong direction of his strivings. *Crime and Punishment* is not a detective novel about the pursuit, capture, confession and legal punishment of a criminal, but a philo-

"*Toward Regeneration*" [*Editor's title*]. *Excerpts from an essay "O filosofsko-eticheskoj problematike romana* Prestuplenie i nakazanie" ["*Philosophical and Ethical Problems in* Crime and Punishment" *by Jurij F. Karjakin in* Dostoevskij i ego vremja [Dostoevsky and his Time], *eds. B. G. Bazanov and G. M. Fridlender (Leningrad, 1971), pp. 176– 188. Translated from the Russian by Robert Louis Jackson.*

sophical, psychological novel about the difficulties of repentance and how to overcome them. . . .

It is essential to note that until the epilogue itself Raskolnikov will only confess to the murder, but not repent of it. He goes to confess not only without a feeling of repentance, but even fortified by a sense of his "rightness." . . . Marx wrote that "shame already is a revolution." A people that has become fouled in slavery and vice must become frightened of itself before it can muster its inner courage. The same is true of the individual; yet right up to the epilogue Raskolnikov is not frightened of himself; he only admires himself more intensely. . . .

In Svidrigailov and Luzhin, whom he hates, Raskolnikov recognizes himself but is afraid to admit the image. They are his doubles, negative doubles, so to speak, who embody all that is bad in him. He looks into them as into a mirror and is ready to cut them down. He is drawn to them and repelled by them. He would like to regard them as caricatures of himself but gradually, though reluctantly, comes to realize that his own "cursed dream" is grotesque and terrible. . . . Still another double of Raskolnikov is Porfiry. Despite all his splendid and well-aimed shots at Raskolnikov, the reader barely masters his dislike of him: Porfiry pursues Raskolnikov like a sadist, with real mockery. A broken man, also, he jeers at others and at himself. He is too restless for the role of wise man or even of moral preceptor. Just because in certain aspects he is an abortive Raskolnikov, he has a keen understanding of him and is vengeful in his attitude toward him. . . .

At the outset, neither Luzhin nor Svidrigailov nor Porfiry can influence Raskolnikov—quite the contrary; but all the same they help lay the groundwork for that crisis in prison when he will recall his terrible dreams. This crisis, though, is prepared by others as well. In order that a man not merely acknowledge, but also repent of his crime and expiate it, he needs positive help. He must have something in himself which can give confidence both to him and to others who would recognize his humanity and wish to help him rise again. Alone, withdrawn into himself, cut off from others, a man who has committed a crime cannot be reborn: this was the realistic and deeply social idea of Dostoevsky.

Raskolnikov's repentance would have been impossible had it not been for other "positive" doubles near him, for other "mirrors" into which he could look to discover all that was good and human in himself. Without people who loved him for the things really worth loving in him, Raskolnikov might just have gone mad or, like Svidrigailov, have killed himself.

The first among these people is Raskolnikov's mother. . . . She is one of the main heroes of the novel. True, only a very few pages are given over to her (the reading of the mother's letter, three meetings with her, his thoughts about her in the epilogue). But her main importance lies in the fact that *Crime and Punishment* is among other things a novel about matricide: it is just because of her son's crime that the mother falls spiritually ill and dies. The son is aware of this fact. Even in his own moments of self-affirmation he certainly did not desire this outcome. The mother more than anyone helps the son to repent and save himself. He is aware of this fact, too. His mother was right when she said to him: "If I had written you the whole truth, you would certainly have abandoned everything and come to us, on foot if need be, for I know your character and feelings, and you would not have let your sister be insulted." And bidding his mother farewell, he, too, was right when he said to her:

> "Mama, dear, no matter what you had heard about me, what people said to you about me—would you still love me as you do now?" He asked this all of a sudden, as if it flowed out of him, as if not thinking about his words or weighing them. "Rodia, what's wrong with you, Rodia? How can you even ask such questions! Who is going to say anything to me about you? Anyway, whoever came to me, I wouldn't believe anybody—I'd simply chase them away." "I came to assure you that I've always loved you, and I'm glad we're alone, even that Dunia's not here," he continued, carried away by the same impulse. "I came to tell you frankly: you won't be happy, but you should know your son loves you right now more than he does himself; and everything you've thought about me—that I'm cruel and don't love you—it was unjust. I'll never stop loving you." . . . Yes, he was glad nobody was there and he was alone with his mother. It seemed as if all that terrible time his heart had softened at once. He fell down before her and kissed her feet. The two of them embraced and wept. (VI, 7)

Only a person criminal in nature or incurably unhappy has not experienced such moments or has not at least wished for them.

Significantly, Raskolnikov says to Sonia: "I asked you yesterday to go with me because you're the only one I have left. . . . I asked you for one thing only, I came for one thing only: don't leave me. You won't leave me, will you, Sonia?" Significantly, too, before the confession "Raskolnikov sensed and understood, once and for all, that Sonia would be with him always from now on, and would follow him to the ends of the earth, wherever fate might send him. His heart heaved." These people bind him to life with living bonds.

Another detail is often overlooked. In his last conversation with his sister, Raskolnikov suddenly takes out a portrait of his deceased fiancée. "I used to talk to her a lot. *About that,* too," he said pensively. "To her alone I confided a lot that later came terribly true. Don't fret"—he looked at Dunia—"she didn't agree, just as you didn't, and I'm glad she's not here." In other words, she too held him back from the crime. Had she been there he might not have decided to "transgress."

Razumikhin also influences Raskolnikov positively and is himself attracted to the Raskolnikov who is on the side of life. This "busybody," as he is sometimes called, is not so limited or unimportant a character as one might suppose. In some respects he is superior to Raskolnikov, for he understands with his mind and heart that one cannot violate the living life; he understands that love for humanity divorced from tangible help to real people is deception and self-deception. He opposes those for whom

> nature doesn't count; nature gets chased away; nature's not supposed to exist! They won't have mankind developing along some *living* historical path to the end, turning finally of itself into normal society; but on the contrary, a social system emerging from some kind of mathematical brain that's going to reconstruct mankind and make it in one moment righteous and sinless, quicker than any life process, no living or historical process needed! . . . That's also why they don't like the life process. A *living soul* isn't called for. A living soul demands life; a living soul doesn't obey mechanical laws; a living soul is suspect; a living soul is retrograde! And this thing here, maybe it reeks of carrion, maybe it's made out of rubber; anyway, it's not alive, it doesn't have a will of its own; anyway, it's servile and won't rebel! And in the long run it turns out everything boils down to how you lay the bricks, how you arrange the rooms and corridors in a phalanstery! The phalanstery's all set, but nature's not quite ready for the phalanstery. Nature wants life, the life process isn't over yet, too early for the graveyard! You can't vault over nature with logic alone. Logic can anticipate three possibilities—but there are a million! The easiest way to solve the problem is to cut short the million and reduce everything to the problem of comfort alone! Temptingly clear, no need to think! That's the main point, having no need to think! The life secret crammed into eight pages! (III, 5)

This thought could refer also to Raskolnikov who could not anticipate even one possibility with his "logic," and when he confronted a million possibilities (the last dream) he finally sent all this logic to the winds.

For the sake of his "dream" Raskolnikov wants to stifle his conscience, crush everything human in himself; but he is unable to do so. Thus, he comes out in defense of a girl pursued by some fop who reminds him of Svidrigailov, then suddenly reflects: "Why the hell did I have to butt in! Is it my business to help? Suppose they swallow each other alive, what's it to me?" Again, he is prepared finally to carry out the crime, but his whole nature protests against its "logic," protests even unconsciously, as in the dream in which, as a boy, he watches as drunken people beat a horse to death. His feelings just immediately after the murder of Lizaveta reflect the same protest:

> Panic was taking hold of him more and more, especially after this, the second and quite unexpected murder. . . . If at that moment he had been in condition to choose rationally or to see more clearly, if he could have imagined all the difficulties of his situation, how altogether desperate, hideous, and absurd it was, and if at the same time he could have grasped how many difficulties he would still have to overcome, how many villainies he might perhaps still have to commit, in order to get out of there, in order to get himself as far as home—quite likely he would have abandoned

everything and gone immediately to give himself up, and not because he was afraid for himself, but entirely for horror and disgust at what he had done. (I, 7)

And now, two days after the murder, he decides to help the Marmeladovs and, after giving them his last pennies, he leaves:

He descended calmly, without haste; feverish, but unaware of it; full of a single immense new sensation of abundant, powerful life surging up in him. This sensation could be compared to the sensation of a man condemned to death who is suddenly and unexpectedly pardoned. (II, 7)

It is the same Raskolnikov who rescued some children from a fire, who gave assistance to a student and his father. We may also recall the scene of reconciliation with Dunia about which Razumikhin rightly said: "That's what I like about him! . . . He has these—gestures."

It is just such a "gesture," too, when, fearing that Svidrigailov who knows his secret, might use it as a weapon against his sister, Raskolnikov reflects that "in order to divert Dunia from some possible rash step he might, perhaps, have to give himself up." (VI, 3) This follows not long after he has said to Sonia: "You laid hands on yourself, you took a life . . . *your own* (what's the difference!)." (IV, 4) It turned out that there was a "difference."

Svidrigailov correctly senses not only "something in common" between them but also a striking difference: "I understand the kind of moral problem that must be bothering you. Moral problems, eh? The man and the citizen: that kind of problem? You should forget it. What good does it do you now? He-he. You mean, for all that, you're still a man and a citizen? If that's the way it goes, you shouldn't have started something that wasn't really your style. I suppose you could shoot yourself. Or don't you feel like it?" (VI, 5) Sonia is also right when she says to him: "But how could you—a man like you? How could you bring yourself to do such a thing?" (V, 4) Razumikhin sums up Raskolnikov this way: "He's morose, gloomy, haughty, and proud. . . . He's magnanimous and kind . . . as though he had two contradictory characters that keep changing places." These two "irreconcilable characters" appear in the following passage: "All at once he felt a strange, unexpected sensation, a kind of bitter hatred for Sonia. As if he were himself surprised and frightened by the feeling, he suddenly raised his head and looked at her intently; her disturbed and painfully troubled gaze rested upon him. There was love in that look. His hatred disappeared like a phantom." (V, 4)

The irreconcilable nature of the contradiction appears at the very beginning when Raskolnikov speaks of his "cursed dream." The dream is tempting, attractive, but nonetheless "cursed" . . . The contradiction, seemingly is insoluble: he must either view the dream as not cursed, or renounce it altogether. . . . When Raskolnikov yields to base impulses he maliciously laughs (though not without self-laceration) at his own magnanimity—it is just Schilleresque rhetoric, he thinks; and he vows not to yield to it in the future. But when (at first only briefly) he nonetheless yields to positive impulses he also acts accordingly, with passion and again with self-laceration, and wants to renounce his "cursed dream."

No matter whether he is providing a theoretical groundwork for the crime, or carrying it out, or seeking to rationalize it, he is nonetheless at the same time violating his true nature, compelling himself to act in contradiction to it. But when he gives embodiment to those "gestures" (of which Razumikhin speaks) he acts naturally, organically, and expands with affirmative, not somber exaltation. There is, was, and will be born in him a dream, not a "cursed" one, but one which even his mother would bless.

This interweaving of opposing aims, this struggle of irreconcilable motifs, emerges impressively in Raskolnikov's last meeting with his sister Dunia:

> "I am going to give myself up now. But I don't know why I am going to give myself up." . . . "By going to suffer, surely you wash away half your crime?" she cried, pressing and hugging and kissing him. "Crime? What crime?" he suddenly shouted, in a kind of sudden rage. "Killing a foul, noxious louse! An old pawnbroker woman no good to anybody, who sucked the life juices of the poor—why, for killing her I'll be forgiven forty sins! I don't think about it, and I don't think about washing it away. Why does everybody push 'crime, crime!' at me? Only now do I see clearly the full absurdity of my cowardliness, now that I've already decided to accept this unnecessary shame! Just because I'm worthless and have no talent, maybe also for my own advantage, as—Porfiry—suggested! . . . I never, never realized this more clearly than now, and I understand my crime less than ever! I have never, never felt stronger or more convinced than now!"
> (VI, 7)

And right after these words we read:

> The color even returned to his pale, exhausted face. In the middle of his last outburst, however, his eyes desperately met Dunia's; and he found in that look so much anguish for him that involuntarily he came to his senses. Anyway you looked at it, he felt, he had made these two poor women miserable. Anyway you looked at it, he had been the cause. "Dunia, darling! If I'm guilty, forgive me. Though if I'm guilty, I cannot be forgiven. Good-bye! Let's not quarrel. It's time—it's high time. Don't follow me, I beg you; I still have a call to make. You go now, and stay with Mother. I beg you to! It's the last and the greatest request I have to make of you. Don't ever leave her. When I said good-bye to her, she was in such anxiety I don't think she can bear it—she'll die or go out of her mind. Be with her! Razumikhin will be with you both. I spoke to him. Don't weep for me. I'll try to be brave and honest as long as I live, even though I'm a murderer. Maybe you'll hear my name sometime. I won't disgrace you; you'll see. I may yet prove—well, good-bye for now." (VI, 7)

But on parting from his sister he once again wants to liberate himself from the spectre of this love: "I'm wicked, I see that . . . But why do they have to love me so if I'm not worth it?" (In other words, there is some "worth" in him!) "If only I were alone and nobody loved me and I never loved anybody! *All this wouldn't have happened!*" (VI, 7) That is, he would have felt no pangs of conscience. Things would have been different: he might have done anything, disregarded every obstacle.

If there is no conscience, all is permissible, all evil is permissible. If there is conscience, all is also permissible, and all good is permissible: this, it appears, is the logic of Dostoevsky. It is a long time before this logic wins over Raskolnikov. He becomes even more set in his "arithmetrical" convictions at the beginning of his imprisonment. . . .

> It was not the horrors of convict life, the hard work or the food or the shaved head or the ragged clothes which broke him. What did he care about these sufferings and torments! . . . His pride was deeply wounded, and it was from wounded pride that he took sick. . . . If only fate had granted him remorse—searing remorse, shattering the heart, banishing sleep—the kind of remorse with terrible pangs that conjure up the noose and the whirlpool! He would have rejoiced! Agony and tears—that, too, is life! But he felt no remorse for his crime. . . . There was only one sense in which he acknowledged his transgression: simply that he hadn't followed it through, and had gone and confessed. (Epilogue, 2)

Raskolnikov repents after his painful anxiety over the fate of his mother, after he recognizes that she had fallen ill and died because of him . . . He repents after Sonia follows him to prison, after he had scornfully turned away from her, all the while that she was patiently bearing everything and awaiting the "moment." He repents after he becomes aware of that fearful and impassable gulf that lies between him and the other convicts. They had regarded him with ill-will, hated him and once almost killed him. They cried out to him: "You're an atheist! You don't believe in God!" they shouted at him. "You should be killed!" But in reality it was not his "atheism" for which they hated him. Though they had not read his articles and were unfamiliar with his theories about two categories of people, they instinctively felt that even in prison he put himself in the "first category," while they (as well as Sonia) were relegated to the "second" category—the herd. It was for this reason that they wanted to kill him. Long ago the drunken Marmeladov had said to him: "Do you understand now, my dear sir, what it means having nowhere to go? No! You wouldn't understand that yet." Much later, paying a heavy price, Raskolnikov understood more fully Marmeladov's words.

Raskolnikov repents after he had originally considered insoluble the question: "Why were they [the convicts] so fond of Sonia?" They were fond of her not so much because she remained a believer but because she remained a believer in people, ready at all times to help them. Raskolnikov repents only after his long illness, after recalling his nightmares.

In those nightmares Raskolnikov's "trichinae," his "cursed dream" escapes and poisons everything and everybody. A world epidemic breaks out.[1] Everybody wants to belong to the "first category" yet to register everyone else in the "second" one. Everybody kills his moneylender, his Lizaveta, his mother, in the name of this idea. Thus Raskolnikov recoils from his "cursed dream" only when he discovers its final consequences on a world scale. Self-will (not freedom) of the individual becomes the condition for the self-will of all. The "dream" leads to doomsday. The little apocalypse (the murder of the old lady, of Lizaveta, the sufferings of the innocent house painter Mikolka, the death of his mother, etc.) concludes with a grand apocalypse. And, at this point, at last, Raskolnikov becomes frightened of himself, and this fright now makes way for the courage which will enable him to renounce his crime. Finally, he repents only when, after his recovery, he meets Sonia on the shore of a broad steppe river:

> He did not know himself how it happened, but suddenly something seemed to seize him and hurl him to her feet. He wept and embraced her knees. . . . He loved her infinitely. . . . In those pale, sickly faces there also glowed the light of the renewed future, resurrection to a new life. Love resurrected them. . . . He knew that he was born again. He felt himself completely renewed in his very being. . . . He recalled how he had constantly caused her pain . . . These memories did not grieve him now; he knew the infinite love with which he would redeem her suffering. (Epilogue, 2)

We find in the epilogue, finally, the explanation for that thirst for life (albeit "on a yard of space") which at first Raskolnikov had taken for cowardice and which troubled him:

> He also suffered from another thought: why had he not killed himself at that time? Why had he stood overlooking the river, and preferred, after all, to confess his guilt? Was his desire to live so strong? And was it so hard to overcome? Hadn't Svidrigailov, who feared death, overcome that desire? He posed the question in anguish, and failed to understand that even as he had looked down into the river he had perhaps sensed a profound lie within himself and in his convictions. He did not understand that this feeling might have been a token of the future break in his life, of his future resurrection, his future new view of life. (Epilogue, 2)

The novel concludes with the idea that an even more difficult period lies ahead for Raskolnikov—a period of expiation. "That is the begin-

---

[1] As Valery Kirpotin suggests in his study *Razocharovanie i krushenie Rodiona Raskolnikova* [*Disillusionment and Downfall of Rodion Raskolnikov*] (Moscow, 1970), p. 439, Raskolnikov's "plague" dream may well echo Matthew 24: 3–13. It should be noted, in this connection, that Matthew 24: 8—"all this is but the beginning of sufferings" (Oxford Annotated Bible)—reads in the Russian version: *"Vse zhe eto nachalo boleznej"*—"all this is but the beginning of the afflictions." [ED.]

ning of a new story, though; the story of a man's gradual renewal, the story of his gradual regeneration, of his gradual transition from one world to another, of his acquaintance with a new reality of which he had previously been completely ignorant." Dostoevsky repeats the word "gradually" three times, emphasizes the difficulty Raskolnikov will face in remaking himself. The last paragraph of the novel concludes with the words: "That would make the subject of a new story; our present story is ended." Here we have, in essence, a courageous confession of a major defeat of Dostoevsky as a Christian ideologist, a defeat which turns out to be a major victory for Dostoevsky the artist.

Conscience is born without religion. . . . It was a triumph of artistic sensitivity that Dostoevsky broke off *Crime and Punishment* before Raskolnikov's religious "revelation." That revelation is only stated. Dostoevsky lacked the power—the power of religious conviction—to depict his hero's "great deed in the future." . . . There was no religious "remaking" of Raskolnikov. He is resurrected not through religion but through the love of Sonia. Significantly, he confesses to the crime only after he has understood "that Sonia would be with him always from now on, and would follow him to the ends of the earth, wherever fate might send him." (VI, 8) And it is natural that on the morning of his resurrection (in the epilogue) the theme of the sun should sound again: "the boundless steppe flooded with sunshine." It is also not accidental that Svidrigailov's decision to commit suicide . . . becomes irrevocable immediately after he hears the word "never!" from Dunia. (VI, 5) There had been "something in common" between Svidrigailov and Raskolnikov, but it no longer existed. The suicide of one is followed by the resurrection of the other.

The Death of Svidrigailov

by Aron Z. Steinberg

Shatov observes in *The Devils*:

> If a great people does not believe that truth resides with it alone (just so—
> with it alone and exclusively); if this people does not believe that it alone
> is fit and destined to resurrect and save everybody by its truth, then it must
> at once be transformed into ethnographical material, and no longer be a
> great people. A truly great people can never reconcile itself to playing a
> secondary role among mankind, nor even one of the first, but always and
> exclusively must play the leading role. (Part II, chap. 1, sect. vii)

How strange these words sound! They seem to echo out of the depths
of the ages, out of the hoary times of the Old Testament; indeed, it seems
as if these words are spoken not by a Russian about the Russian people,
but by a Biblical soothsayer about his native Israel. And, indeed, for
Shatov-Dostoevsky the God-bearing Russian people is in essence now the
resurrected Israel. One need only recall the words uttered by Shatov:

> Every people is only a people so long as it has its own special god and
> excludes all other gods in the world irreconcilably; so long as it believes
> that by its own god it will conquer and drive out from the world all other
> gods. That has been the belief from the very beginning of time, of all
> great peoples, at any rate, of all who have in any way been remarkable, all
> who have been leaders of humanity. There's no going against the facts. The
> Jews lived only to await the coming of the true God and to bequeath the
> true God to the world. (Part II, ch. 1, sect. vii)

"A Jew without God is somehow unthinkable; a Jew without God is
inconceivable," Dostoevsky says himself in his *Diary of a Writer*. (March,
1877, chap. 2, sect. i)

Now, here Dostoevsky comes up against a stubborn contradiction. It
seems that he has inherited his central idea—his messianism, his faith
in the God-bearing Russian people, in the religion of the "Russian God"
(that is Dostoevsky's phrase in a letter to A. Maikov)—from the Jewish people, from that grand monument of ancient times, the Bible. Then all of
a sudden, out of the clear blue, he is confronted by the puny, excruciat-

---

"The Death of Svidrigailov" [*Editor's title*]. *Excerpt from "Dostoevskij i evrejstvo"*
[*"Dostoevsky and Jewry"*], *by Aron Z. Steinberg, in* Versty *no. 3 (Paris 1928):108–5.
Translated from the Russian by Robert Louis Jackson.*

ingly comic image of the convict "Isaika" [the Jew Isay Fomich Bumshtein
in *Notes from the House of the Dead*—ED.] who cries out boldly at the
top of his lungs: "What do you mean—inherited? By what right? What
about me? Do you mean that I don't even exist?" "But there is only one
truth," Dostoevsky retorts in a rage, "and therefore only one of the people can have the true God." Therefore—we may continue this thought
on our own: it's either we, Russians, or you, Jews; or, to be more exact:
the true Israel today is the Russian people. If the Russian people but
once renounces the faith that it alone has just claim to the centuries-old
messianic idea of the Old Testament Jews, if this faith wavers but once
the Russian people will forthwith disintegrate, crumble, dissolve into
ethnographical material. But the reverse is also true: if the historical
truth, the future and salvation of the whole human race has been en-
trusted by Providence to Russia and Russians, then all those Jews still
wandering the world are but historical dust—"Yids, Jewkins." [1] From a
little episode in *Crime and Punishment* (VI, 6) that often passes unno-
ticed, the attentive reader will see how this conclusion logically and in-
escapably follows for Dostoevsky.

When Svidrigailov makes his final decision to commit suicide and goes
out onto a filthy Petersburg bridge to put an end to his life in the presence of "an official witness," his attention is riveted on a sentry patrolling
before a watchtower, a little man. "Wrapped in a gray army coat, he was
wearing a brass 'Achilles' helmet' on his head. His sleepy glance rested
coldly on Svidrigailov as he approached. His face bore that eternal pee-
vish woebegone look which is irrevocably stamped on every Jewish face
without exception. For some time Svidrigailov and Achilles looked at each
other in silence." Svidrigailov takes out his revolver while the mythical
hero who has risen out of the thick damp fog lisps unceasingly: "Nu, vat
you vont—ah? . . . Diss ain't de place." But what cares Svidrigailov for
the nasal words of caution from a frail Achilles: he pulls the trigger and
a shot rings out.

This episode, Svidrigailov's painful farewell to life, may strike us at
first as some kind of hopeless enigma; yet it must be remembered that not
a single scene, image or word in Dostoevsky, particularly in his most finished works, is without a more profound and allegorical meaning. Indeed, this enigma is easily unravelled as soon as one compares the "idea"
of Svidrigailov with Dostoevsky's own view on the essence of Jewry.
Svidrigailov is outraged at the idea of eternity and immortality—to him
a kind of bad infinity—and he rebels against the eternal "mark time,"
against the eternal return. Now what encounter could more graphically
sum up for him all the senselessness of existence for the sake of mere
naked existence than a meeting with the centuries old spectre-like Jew,

---

[1] Steinberg, of course, invents this little dialogue between "Isaika" and Dostoevsky.
For a discussion of Dostoevsky's characterization of Isay Fomich Bumshtein see my article, "A Footnote to *Selo Stepanchikovo*" in *Ricerche Slavistiche*, 17 (1970–1973). [ED.]

the Eternal Jew! Like a puppet he drones out endlessly to the world his "diss ain't de place": not the place to die, not the place to rebel against the "law" of life and its immutability. Now spectres may woefully take satisfaction in this kind of negative affirmation of life, but a truly living person [in Dostoevsky's view] will prefer total self-destruction to this cursed form of self-preservation. Not he who is drawn by his God like a mute sacrifice, but only he who himself prepares the path for Him, for the anointed Savior, has the duty and right to live.

Thus, Dostoevsky's "anti-Semitism" is revealed to us as the reverse side —and true foundation—of his own "Judaism." The apparent contradiction is in fact rectilinear, iron logic.

The Death of Marmeladov

by Konrad Onasch

Konstantin Leontiev,[1] sombre and unpoetic, realized that a person like Sonia is ill-adapted not only to Russian Orthodoxy but indeed to any Christian dogma; she represents in fact the pious soul emancipated from both church and dogma. One sentence in Dostoevsky's "symbol of faith" credo describes Sonia's position exactly: "Even if somebody proved to me that Christ was outside the truth, and it *really* was true that the truth was outside Christ, then I would rather remain with Christ than with the truth." [2] By "truth" here Dostoevsky undoubtedly had in mind Christian dogma. It is possible, then, for Sonia, as in Schleiermacher's theology of "feeling" and "consciousness" to stand with Christ as the embodiment of all that is good and noble in man, quite apart from the truth and teachings of the church. . . .

It is well known that church and dogma play no role in Dostoevsky's work, though a few scenes in *Notes from the House of the Dead* may have some relevance to them. In *Crime and Punishment,* however, we are confronted directly with a moving encounter between the pious soul and the church—from which, despite her participation in its rituals, she is nonetheless inwardly emancipated. The scene is that of the dying Marmeladov. . . .

The death of the ecstatic drunkard Marmeladov is described in chapter 7, Part II of *Crime and Punishment.* He has been run down by a horse and carriage. Raskolnikov carries him into his wretched flat. Dostoevsky depicts his death with consummate artistry. . . . Marmeladov's death is marked by unusual agitation and unseemliness: the room is crowded with curiosity-seekers, cigarettes dangling perpetually from their lips; with police officials; with a continual bustling in and out; with the whimpering of Marmeladov's children and the frightful wheezing, dry cough of his wife. All the indescribable misery of phantasmagoric Petersburg

"*The Death of Marmeladov*" [*Editor's title*]. From Dostojewski als Verführer *by Konrad Onasch (Zurich: EVZ—Verlag, 1961), pp. 73, 77–80. Reprinted by permission of the author. Translated from the German by Robert Louis Jackson.*

[1] Konstantin Leontiev (1831–91), Russian writer and literary critic, accused Dostoevsky and Tolstoy in 1882 of deviating from Orthodoxy, of offering a "rose-colored Christianity." [ED.]

[2] From a letter of Dostoevsky to N. D. Fon-Vizina, February, 1854. [ED.]

seems to have been concentrated in this room. Besides the doctor, a priest has been sent for: the dying man himself made the request. "The priest appeared in the doorway with the Sacrament. He was a gray little old man." After the confession and extreme unction a conversation takes place between the priest and an embittered Katerina Ivanovna who is completely upset and distraught. Dostoevsky's characterization of the priest is entirely devoid of irony. He is, indeed, perhaps the only real person in this fantastic throng of human spectres. A cleric who has grown gray in service, he is only doing his duty. He says what he has probably said countless times in these circumstances: "God is merciful, look to the Almighty for help." Katerina Ivanovna reacts bitterly, though, when the priest bids her forgive her dying husband. " 'Eh, Father! Those are words, just words! Forgive! . . . What's this talk about forgiveness! As it is, I have forgiven!' A deep and terrible coughing fit interrupted her words. She coughed up into her handkerchief and thrust it at the priest to show him as she clutched her chest with the other hand. The handkerchief was covered with blood. The priest bowed his head and said nothing." At this very moment, in fact, when Katerina Ivanovna with the children against the background of the crowd has knelt for the confession, a quiet power enters—*the* opponent of an organized, hierarchical church which rules dogma, souls and lands: *homo religiosa;* just *how* this power makes its appearance is breath-taking:

> Then timidly and inaudibly a girl squeezed through the crowd. Strange indeed was her sudden appearance in that room, in the middle of beggary, rags, death and desperation. She, too, was in rags. She was cheaply dressed, but tricked out gutter-fashion, according to the rules and taste of that special world whose shameful purpose was all too apparent. Sonia paused on the landing, right on the threshold. She did not cross the threshold, though, and looked like some lost soul, oblivious of everything, it seemed, unconscious of her fourth-hand gaudy silk dress with its long absurd train and the immense crinoline that filled the entire doorway, so inappropriate here, and her bright-colored shoes, and the parasol she scarcely needed at night, but which she took with her, and her foolish round straw hat with the bright red feather on top. From under this hat, which was cocked at a rakish angle, gazed a thin, pale, frightened little face, with parted lips and eyes immobile in terror. Sonia was a small, thin girl of about eighteen, fairly pretty, blonde, with remarkable blue eyes. (II, 7)

Once again we encounter the "grotesque." It is not necessary to realize at once that the bright red feather on Sonia's hat recalls the red feather on Mephistopheles' hat in order to grasp the daring alienating effect of this strange juxtaposition. Marmeladov breathes his last in the arms of this alienated girl, this religious soul. Katerina Ivanovna, who cannot forgive her husband, speaks almost (or perhaps even consciously) in defiance of Christ's last words on the cross: "He's got his!" I know of no other scene in nineteenth-century literature in which true religiosity and

organized religion are more vividly set off against each other than here;
but its genius will only reveal itself to one who has first thoroughly
grasped and analyzed the elaborate contrasts and intricate style of the
grotesque—this intermingling of eros and religion.

Life and death are closely intertwined. Thus, in *Anna Karenina* Tolstoy chooses the moment of the death of Nikolai, Levin's brother, to
have Kitty feel that new life is stirring within her. . . . With Dostoevsky
the hour of Marmeladov's death signals the inner spiritual birth of the
new man Raskolnikov. He sees Sonia for the first time and begins to love
her. Once again this happening is marked by inimitable contrasts, once
again true religion and church are juxtaposed:

> He descended [the stairs] calmly, without haste; feverish, but unaware of
> it; full of a single immense new sensation of abundant, powerful life surg-
> ing up in him. This sensation could be compared to the sensation of a man
> condemned to death who is suddenly and unexpectedly pardoned. Halfway
> down the stairs the priest, who was on his way, overtook him. Raskolnikov
> let him go by in silence, merely exchanging a silent bow. (II, 7)

These few sentences are elaborately polished: in the Russian text a
peculiar parallel exists to the earlier appearance of Sonia, a parallel
which involves not only certain phrases and sentence structures, but also
sounds. The typical Dostoevsky word "suddenly" is heard twice: the melody of new life begins imperceptibly, just as Sonia enters the room and
Raskolnikov goes down the steps. In another equally striking contrast,
the allusion to Dostoevsky's death sentence echoes here[3] (one may compare this with Myshkin's comments in chapter 5, Part I of *The Idiot*);
but the triumphant melody of life has begun; it leads Raskolnikov past
the priest even with a certain respect. It leads him to Sonia. With Sonia
the seven years of punishment will go by like the seven great splendid
days of God's Creation:

> Blüh auf, gefröner Christ,
> Der Mai ist vor der Tür!
> Du bleibest ewig tot,
> Blühst du nicht jetzt und hier! [4]

[3] Dostoevsky was condemned to death for his participation in the Petrashevsky reading circle in 1849. On the field of execution the death sentence was commuted to eight
years of imprisonment and exile. His sense of joy with *life* again is conveyed in his
extraordinary letter to his brother, December 22, 1849, a few hours after the reprieve.
[ED.]

[4] The lines are from the Swiss writer Gottfried Keller (1819–90). "Blossom forth,
frozen Christ/May is at hand!/You will remain forever dead/If you do not blossom
forth here and now!"

Disease as Dialectic in *Crime and Punishment*

by James M. Holquist

Disease has never been the exclusive province of doctors. It has been used as a matter for speculation and illustration by poets and prophets from the Theban plague of Sophocles to the Algerian plague of Camus. Health has been seen as a norm (even by those, like Pascal, who saw illness as a possible good) from which disease was an unnatural departure. Unnatural and inhuman—something occasioned by Gods or demons. Disease for many societies has been the most frequent evidence of God's will at work in the world, and Camus has shown that even in his secular city of Oran, rats can still instruct. The equation of bodily with spiritual health is an ancient one; exorcising chants are the only poetry of some tribes. And the same question is at the core of many of the greatest poems (such as Mallarmé's *Fenêtres*) and stories (such as Kafka's *Metamorphosis*) of our time and culture. But it is in the novels of Dostoevsky that the theme would seem to find its most insistent and allusive treatment.

Notes from the Underground has as its first line, "I am a sick man," and in this, as in so many other things, this work prefigures the concerns of Dostoevsky's great post-Siberian phase. The fact that *The Devils (Besy)* is usually rendered in English as *The Possessed* is simply eponymous confirmation of the central role possession plays in that novel. *The Idiot* is an exercise in the ambiguities of another type of possession, as, with regard to Smerdyakov and Ivan, is *The Brothers Karamazov*. Dostoevsky himself, as is well known, was an epileptic; but such critics as Mihailovsky and Gorky, when they called Dostoevsky unhealthy, did so not because of his *physical* affliction. Like Claudel, when he calls Pascal a sick man, they intend a much more sweeping indictment. Dostoevsky is for them sick because he is so obsessively taken up with afflictions of all kinds, from the implicit threat, raised by the many prostitutes in his fiction, of syphilis, to the varieties of mental disorder explicit in all the novels. What such a view fails to take into account is that these are spiritual—or better, philosophical, even more than physical or mental disabilities. Dmitry Karamazov says the heart of man is a battlefield for God and the Devil, but in fact for Dostoevsky *all* the organs of the body constitute such a battlefield. This can be more precisely seen in *Crime and Punishment*.

The novel's narrative movement is as much that of an argument as it is that of a mere story. The two poles of the debate, as always in Dostoevsky, are good and evil. But as the distinguished theologian Reinhold Niebuhr reminds us, "the mystery of good and evil in human life and in the world cannot be completely comprehended as stated in perfectly logical terms." [1] Dostoevsky advances his opposition of the two by means of a series of complex substitutions. Thus the danger of a Manichean abstractness is avoided when good and evil are made present first of all as a conflict between two competing soteriologies or theories of salvation: Raskolnikov's antitranscendent "supermanism" on the one hand, and Sonia's Christian redemption on the other. These two systems are further particularized in the characters who espouse them, of course. But the dynamic structure which is most responsible for the clash and movement of the oppositions results from Dostoevsky-as-narrator's subtle shaping of disease motifs.

Crime and Punishment is, then, a series of oppositions which are united into a meaningful whole by disease symbolism: its progression, both as argument and as story, is akin to the etiology of certain diseases, whose true nature can be determined only after they have run their full course; their defining symptom is their last symptom chronologically to appear. For the specific quality of the disease which permeates the novel is made evident only in the last pages of the epilogue. The epilogue to *Crime and Punishment* is one of the hottest areas of dispute in Dostoevsky criticism, the quarrel usually centering on whether Raskolnikov is "cured" or not, i.e., whether, in the face of all that has gone before, the narrator's assurances that Raskolnikov has found salvation are justified. This is a point to which I will return later, but for now suffice it to say that the epilogue is assumed to be a crucial addition to the main text for the reason just cited: it provides the key to the pathology which is the subject of the novel.

This key is found in the dream Raskolnikov has while (fittingly enough) in the prison hospital, the famous dream of the strange microbes which arise out of Asia:

> Men attacked by them became at once mad and furious. But never had men considered themselves so intellectual and so completely in possession of the truth as these sufferers, never had they considered their decisions, their "scientific" conclusions, their "moral" convictions so "infallible." Whole villages, whole towns and peoples went mad from the infection. All were excited and did not understand one another. Each thought that he alone had the truth . . . men killed each other in senseless spite . . . the tocsin rang all day long in the towns . . . all men and all things were in-

---

[1] Reinhold Niebuhr, "The Truth in Myths," *The Nature of Religious Experience*, [Douglas Clyde Macintosh Festschrift], eds. Bewkes et al. (New York: Harper & Bros., 1937), pp. 124–25.

volved in destruction. The plague spread and moved further and further. (Epilogue, 2) [2]

This vision is analogous to a Platonic myth in that it raises the action of the whole novel to another, more schematic level. It is a legend both in the sense that it is a tale of wonderful events, and in the sense that it is key to the symbols in the map of human possibilities constituted by the preceding six books. The bearers of the disease are usually translated as microbes; but in the Russian text *trixiny,* trichinae, which are, of course, associated in pathology with pigs, or swine. This, coupled with the fact that we know Dostoevsky will take the title of a later novel from the Biblical parable of the Gadarene swine, suggests that the disease is not only physical, or more correctly, mental, but spiritual. It is both psychopathology and possession, a neat metaphor for the two levels, intellectual and religious, on which the plot advances simultaneously.

I am assuming that this dream defines the larger plot of the novel. But this larger plot is cast in the form of a novel, so we must seek terms appropriate to a novel's greater degree of contingency, if we are to see its pattern. That is, *Crime and Punishment* is about crime and punishment, but these are only the effects of another dynamic; namely, contagion, disease, immunity, and cure. The contagion and disease are associated with the *secular* myth of rationalism; immunity and cure with the *Christian* myth of redemption.

Another way of putting it is to say that all the characters in the novel are sick in varying degrees, except for Sonia, Razumikhin, and Porfiry Petrovich (although they may be carriers of a sort) and the degree to which a given character is diseased is what will define the enormity of his crime, i.e., his position in the rhetoric of good versus evil, redemption versus mere progress. There is a hierarchy here: from Svidrigailov at the bottom, to Sonia at the top. Raskolnikov's story is his movement from the sickness of the one to the health of the other. In the ocean which separates the two poles of the opposition float the storm-tossed flotsam and jetsam of the minor characters. We shall not, in the present essay, find space to discuss them, but they are merely ambulatory cases, the out-patients. What of those who are in the last throes of disease, such as Svidrigailov or Raskolnikov? It is in connection with the two most advanced cases of the disease, that the other possibilities of the microbe dream—immunity and cure—come into play. That is, in the dream not *everyone* is affected: "Only a few men could be saved in the whole world. They were a pure, chosen people, destined to found a new race and a new life, to renew and purify the earth." The epidemiology of the most virulent form of this disease, as in any other, cannot be understood without taking into account the reasons why some exposed subjects do not contract it. What

[2] From the Constance Garnett translation of *Crime and Punishment* (New York: Airmont Publishing Co., Inc., 1967).

this means in terms of the text is that Svidrigailov's and Raskolnikov's fates are integrally related to possibilities of cure, or redemption, represented by such other characters as Porfiry Petrovich, Razumikhin, and pre-eminently, Sonia Marmeladov.

Disease is a kind of discourse. English recognizes this by defining epidemiology as the study of *communicable* diseases. That is, you *get* disease from someone else, and you *pass it on* to someone else. With this in mind, we can set up something like a grammar of infection for Svidrigailov. The cause of his illness is history. Like Raskolnikov, to whom he is constantly compared, he is a *modern* case, religion has developed into superstition (he believes in ghosts but not God). He commits crimes against the family when he murders his wife, and against society in his frequent seductions. His delusion is that for him there are no laws. Dostoevsky's later equation, "Without God all is permitted," is in Svidrigailov already fully realized. The consequences of this are manifold. He is, first of all, definitive answer to Raskolnikov's theory of the lawgiver (Solon, Mahomet, Napoleon) as lawbreaker. For Svidrigailov, because he sees himself as above the law, breaks it consistently—and yet he is the very anti-thesis of Raskolnikov's exalted image of the great criminal; far from being a Napoleon, he is a bored cardsharp whose smallness is dramatized in his reductive conception of eternity as a spider-infested outhouse. It is the disparity between the grandiose conception of what it means to be above the law, and the ugly reality in which this conception results; that is, as in so many other ways, Svidrigailov embodies the logical consequences of Raskolnikov's confusion.

Svidrigailov's metaphysical illness has its bodily counterpart in his abnormal sex life; Rasholnikov makes this explicit when he calls Svidrigailov's lechery a disease (VI, 3). This is the means by which Svidrigailov's powers of infection are realized; he literally corrupts several young girls, either by physically raping them (giving a sinister twist to his statement that his "only hope is anatomy") or by violating their imaginations (as in the case of his 16-year-old fiancée who "resembles a madonna," thus providing an extra *frisson*).

One of the ways in which Svidrigailov parallels Raskolnikov is in his relationship to a female-saviour. Svidrigailov hopes to save himself by marrying Dunia. But—there can be no cure for so advanced, so modern a case as his. Yet he refuses to see this, and both literally and figuratively invests a good deal in Raskolnikov's sister. He has, like Luzhin, tried to possess her in a number of ways. He begins with the offer of money, and ends with the threat of exposing her brother. It might be thought that he wants to add just another young girl to his list of forcible conquests (although in his perverted canon of taste she differs from other victims by reason of her advanced age—she is, after all, eighteen), or, again like Luzhin, that he simply wants a beautiful young wife. But that something more powerful, more complex is involved here is made clear after Dunia's definitive rejection of him. Svidrigailov says that in refusing him, Dunia is killing him, and this is no more than the literal truth. Up to this point Svidrigailov has wavered between the twin possibilities of marriage (not to his sixteen-year-old fiancée, but to Dunia), and suicide. It is only after Dunia rejects him that he commits himself fully to suicide. The contract with Raskolnikov and Sonia could not be more explicit. Dunia is not the bearer of a force capable of saving Svidrigailov, even if she wanted to do so. For Raskolnikov Sonia comes finally to represent a mystical way larger than Sonia's significance as a mere woman. Because of his perverted sense that there are *only* human beings in the world, unaffected by forces greater than themselves, Svidrigailov believes that Dunia, a mere woman, can save him. The failure of Svidrigailov's attempt at salvation is thus a condemnation of those soteriologies which exclude an extrahistorical transcendent.

It has often been said that *Crime and Punishment* is Dostoevsky's "best made" novel; in the degree to which one basic figure—sickness/health, damnation/salvation, crime/punishment—is at the center of all the patterns of relationship in the novel, this is certainly the case. We have seen that the microbe dream gives structure to the whole narrative, but there is another type of dream in the novel which gives meaning to the career of a particular character. Svidrigailov's final dreams are of this latter sort. The reasons why Dunia's rejection must lead to suicide are contained in the series of dreams Svidrigailov has in the flophouse *after* his last encounter with Dunia. Symbols of death and disease crowd not only these dreams, but the narrative framework which surrounds them, providing yet another example of Dostoevsky's method of fusing realistic and fantastic dream modes. On the night Svidrigailov dreams his final dreams, there is a torrential downpour in the city, the canals are swollen to flooding. The narrator tells us the rats are coming out of their dens (as well Svidrigailov when he emerges to shoot himself). The connection between those rats and the rodent Svidrigailov sees in his first dream are clear— and made even more so when upon awakening Svidrigailov finds a real mouse in his bed. Next he dreams of a dead young girl, one of his many victims: the dream equivalent of his real crimes. Finally, just before he goes out to commit suicide, he dreams of a five-year-old girl, whom he tucks tenderly into bed, only to be revolted by her lascivious smile of sexual invitation. As the microbe dream recapitulates the whole novel, this series of dreams recapitulates Svidrigailov's progressive course toward death. Just before the first dream, he muses to himself, "perhaps Dunia would have made a new man of me, somehow." Immediately he dreams, and then actually sees, a mouse, previously associated with the flood and one of the most common carriers of disease, rats. Svidrigailov is presented as one contaminated. Next we see the effects of his contamination on others—the girl who has drowned herself after having been raped. In the final dream we see the effects of the disease on Svidrigailov himself. De praved as he is, there is no evidence that he ever actually raped a five-year-old child. The thought is so repugnant that even Svidrigailov is repelled, appalled by the smile of the little girl in his dream. For the first time sensuality, his iconic attribute, his disease, as Raskolnikov has called it, occasions revulsion—from this depth of infection there can be no hope of cure or regeneration. Death is the logical consequence of so fatal a disease, and Svidrigailov's next action is to head toward the Little Neva (which he sees in his mind's eye as swollen; he instinctively moves toward the rats), where he shoots himself.

The question often arises in connection with Dostoevsky's novels, who are they most centrally about? In *Crime and Punishment* this is not the case. Rodion Romanovich Raskolnikov is what the novel is about—he is, in a sense, its plot. That is, the pattern I have been attempting to describe is worked out most completely and memorably in the sequence of his thoughts and actions. He too is diseased, he too infects. As Porfiry Petrovich says, the most terrible thing about Raskolnikov's crime is that he commits it out of conscience.

Raskolnikov's illness manifests itself in various ways. At the lowest level there are the narrator's constant reminders that Raskolnikov is physically ill or mentally deranged. But there is also obvious in him the effects of the particular disease of the plague dream; that is, while Raskolnikov is supremely confident that he is in control of the truth, he is in turn controlled by the ideas which constitute this truth. This syndrome can be seen in the disparity between the involuntariness of his actions and the certainty of his convictions from which those actions spring. Raskolnikov does everything in a daze—he cannot believe he will commit the murder he plans. The crime itself is executed in a dreamy state, and succeeds only due to a series of the most gratuitous coincidences (finding the ax, sneaking into the apartment house unobserved, escaping from the two men who come to the moneylender's door after the murder, etc.); he wanders about the city in a semistupor, and is constantly surprised to find himself within sight of a goal—the apartment of Razumikhin, Svidrigailov, etc. He is obviously not in control—the microbes are. But the most unambiguous index of just how sick Raskolnikov really is, of course, is the enormity of his crimes. I emphasize crimes, because the murder of the two women is only the most shocking of several. He has also, like Marmeladov, violated the covenant of the family—first by cutting himself off from his mother and sister, and secondly by driving his mother into madness. She believes her son did not commit the murder, and yet, in her final delirium, her disjointed words "showed that she knew much more about her son's terrible fate than they had supposed."

Raskolnikov has infected his mother, driving her to her ultimate delusion. But he has infected others, including his landlady's daughter. She was a gentle girl, who wished to be a nun. Raskolnikov admits that he did not love her, although he gave her a verbal promise of marriage.

There is a strong suggestion that he was actually interested in obtaining free credit from the mother, more than in the charms of the daughter (II, 1). The girl literally dies of a disease—typhus—and it is not too much to suggest that this is simply another bodily sign of metaphysical contagion. Not only has Raskolnikov treated the girl as part of a commercial transaction (as Luzhin treats Dunia), but later he reveals to Dunia, as he gives her a miniature of the landlady's daughter, that "to her heart I confided much that has subsequently so horribly come to pass." (VI, vii) The girl was appalled—and soon dies.

Lest this be thought too fanciful an interpretation, it should be remembered that Porfiry Petrovich specifically points out Raskolnikov's power to infect. The source here is significant, for within the framework of the crime/disease pattern, Porfiry Petrovich as detective, one who solves crimes, has also the role of physician. His ability to prognosticate what Raskolnikov will do amounts to a prognosis of Raskolnikov's diseased mental condition. Porfiry Petrovich's method is psychological, but he is aware of the philosophical depth in Raskolnikov's malady: "I have guessed how you feel, have I not? Only in that way you'll lose not only your head, but Razumikhin's also; he's too *good* a man for that, as you yourself know. You are ill, and he is good, and your illness is catching for him." (IV, 5) Of course Razumikhin is not corrupted by Raskolnikov; he possesses an immunity which is a necessary condition for all the novel's characters associated with the health/salvation cluster—Sonia, Porfiry Petrovich, and his relative, Razumikhin himself. Much is made of this name in the novel (by Svidrigailov) and in Dostoevsky criticism, the emphasis usually being put in both cases on the fact that it suggests *razum* or reason. But Razumikhin's real name, as he himself says, is Vrazumikhin (II, iii), the association here being with the verb *vrazumit'*—to make somebody understand, to convince, to make one listen to reason. This is an important distinction in light of the fact that at the very core of the novel lies a pattern of opposing delusions, each jockeying to enforce its will on others. Thus the more active, argumentative associations of Vrazumikhin are more fitting in the context of the narrative than bloodless *razum*. Razumikhin is pre-eminently the active man, comically so; his argument by example is enough to save Dunia, but it cannot save Raskolnikov; it is also adequate protection from the infection Porfiry Petrovich sees in Raskolnikov.

Raskolnikov is, then, the most diseased of all the victims in the novel. But the microbe dream also has in it some Europeans untouched by the malady, and hints at some kind of regeneration. This aspect of the dream is present in the novel most unambiguously in the figure of Sonia; that is, if Svidrigailov is the furthest pole of the disease, she is the furthest pole of cure. She is like Dunia in that she has been thrown into the midst of corruption, but remains untouched. Dunia has not been affected by either Luzhin or Svidrigailov. Sonia is immune both from the effects of her trade

—prostitution—and the onslaught of Raskolnikov's virulent attacks on the purity of her belief. There is a sense in which she is both Magdalene and Madonna simultaneously. But she is unlike Dunia, who fails Svidrigailov, in that she does not reject Raskolnikov.

The fact that she represents health, antidote to Raskolnikov, is projected in a series of metaphors and incidents having to do with fresh air and sunlight. Porfiry Petrovich has early in the book told Raskolnikov that what he needs is fresh air; and as Raskolnikov bids farewell to Dunia, just before his confession, the thought of Sonia flashes into his mind. Dunia would not stand by him if she knew of the murder, but Sonia would. In the next line the narrator says, "There was a breath of fresh air from the window." On the next page Raskolnikov says to himself, "With this idiotic, purely physical weakness, depending on the sunset or something, one cannot help doing something stupid." At this point he has not accepted the meaning that fresh air might have for him, but just after this Raskolnikov tells Razumikhin, "Yesterday a man Porfiry Petrovich said to me that what a man needs is fresh air, fresh air, fresh air. I mean to go to him directly and find out what he meant by that." (VI, 1) When Raskolnikov does go to Porfiry Petrovich, the investigator emphasizes that Raskolnikov's crime was an *aberration,* and repeats, "What you need now is fresh air, fresh air, fresh air." (VI, 3) And as Porfiry Petrovich walks away he says, "the evening will be fine, if only we don't have a storm, though it would be a good thing to freshen the air." The storm, of course, comes and it does freshen the air—Svidrigailov, one possibility for the further course of Raskolnikov's development, commits suicide in the night; this possibility eliminated, the way is left open to the other alternative, Sonia's way, the curative way of fresh air. This the narrator reveals when he says the next day ends with a "warm fresh, bright evening; it had cleared up in the morning." (VI, 7)

But the air, in the city, especially in Dostoevsky's Petersburg, is never really fresh. Siberia, and again, especially Dostoevsky's Siberia, is something else. To see the kind of fresh air it represents, it is well to remember that the whole course of Raskolnikov's progress from sickness to health is not only inherent in the microbe dream, but encapsulated in the action of the entire epilogue. Raskolnikov has been physically ill, in the hospital, but now he goes out into the air: it is "warm, a bright day" on which he symbolically kneels before Sonia. (Epilogue, 2)

This act of submission raises the whole question, touched on earlier, of the epilogue's status with regard to the rest of the novel. Is it, as some have argued, a crudely didactic resolution which is inadequate to the complexity of all that has transpired in the preceding sections; or is it, as others have held, the crux of the novel? It will be obvious from the importance I have assigned to the plague dream, that I hold to the latter point of view. And I hope that the reading I have given above is adequate to support the statement that the main body of the novel contains in it all the preparation that such a narrative conclusion demands. Raskolnikov turns finally not to a God from a machine, but a God from the novel.

That there is an animating concept of God present throughout the novel is obvious. But the aim here is not explicitly to identify that God, or his system, which is a problem for the theologians (and they have not been notably lacking in the enthusiasm to tackle it). What concerns us here is the system, rather, of the fiction *Crime and Punishment*. In order to deal with this problem, it is enough to say that the God evoked in the novel is in the most important of his attributes, recognizably the Christian God, with Dostoevsky putting a special emphasis in this novel on the system of salvation contained in the New Testament. But the mode in which Dostoevsky casts this essentially religious subject is fictive, and one of the most important consequences of treating the problem in a realistic *novel* is the muting of absolute values, which thus ensues. This is the point at which the particular relevance the story of Lazarus has within the context of the novel becomes clear. Because it is all very well for the apostles or Christian theologians to write of a miraculous resurrection from death, the mode not only of their belief, but of their expression, is open to marvel. Real life, real death, and actual resurrection are the terms they employ. But the novel, for obvious reasons, demands less absolute terms. The Lazarus tale occurs several times in the novel, always at crucial, symbolic junctures (as do the other elements of conventional Christian symbolism—the crucifixes, Bibles, holy days, etc.); and it gives structure to Raskolnikov's progress toward salvation. But it does this not by means of a simple-minded, one-to-one correspondence between Raskolnikov and Lazarus.

The parallel exists, of course. But it depends less on the simple and unmediated equation of Raskolnikov with Lazarus than on the ability of the evangelical story to provide the ultimate terms: absolute life, death, and resurrection; these terms are represented in the novel by others more widely operative there: sickness and health, which in turn make possible the more novelistically viable terms of mediation—cure. This is what I mean when I suggest that, while *Crime and Punishment* is not in any strict sense a myth, it does advance its plot, makes its points, mythically.

Since few words have been used more often or carelessly than myth, I shall try to be more specific: I am using the term here as it was defined in an early Lévi-Strauss essay.[3] In this view, myth is a particular mode of dialectic, a means for overcoming contradiction: in myth, "two opposite terms with no intermediary always tend to be replaced by two equivalent terms which allow a third one as mediator. Thus the polar opposites 'life' and 'death' are irreconcilable, but if 'agriculture' (which produces grow-

[3] It first appeared in 1958, but I cite the most readily available version of it: Claude Lévi-Strauss, "The Structural Study of Myth," *Structural Anthropology*, trans. Claire Jacobson and Brooke Grundfest Schoepf (New York: Doubleday & Co. [Anchor Book], 1963), pp. 206–31.

ing things) is substituted for 'life,' and 'war' (which causes destruction)
replaces 'death'; the middle term 'hunt' (the provision of food by means
of killing) is engendered." [4] Thus, "the purpose of myth is to provide a
logical model capable of overcoming a contradiction." [5] That is, the
mythic process does not *resolve* contradictions in their own terms—an
impossibility when they are so real as life and death—rather, it puts them
into another dimension, a kind of alogical, but acceptable, homogeneity.

Crime and Punishment advances its oppositions in much the same way.
A diagram of the movement from the irreconcilable poles of life and
death into the mediating term (cure) which disease makes possible might
look something like this:

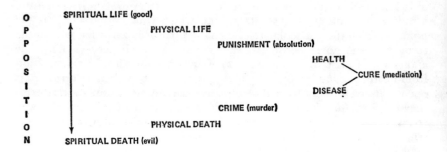

Thus, to return once again to the crucial final lines of the novel: "But
here begins a new story, the story of a man's gradual renewal, the story of
his gradual transfer from one world to another, of his acquaintance with
a new, previously unknown reality." This reality is that of the "new life"
described in the penultimate paragraph of the epilogue. If one conceives
the novel's symbol system as allegorical in the traditional sense, attaching
too strict a religious interpretation to the salvation hinted at, then the
conclusion is hollow and unconvincing. But if one sees in the "new life"
all the implications which the disease/health symbol complex has mythically created in the main body of the novel, the ending does indeed become something like a miracle—a miracle of the novelist's art.

[4] Wayne Shumaker, *Literature and the Irrational* (New York: Washington Square
Press, 1960), p. 129.
[5] Lévi-Strauss, *op. cit.*, p. 226.

Chronology of Important Dates

1821	Fyodor Mikhailovich Dostoevsky born in Moscow, Russia, October 30.
1846	Dostoevsky publishes *Poor Folk*. In his first literary period (1846–49) he publishes, among other works, *The Double, The Landlady, White Nights,* and *Netochka Nezvanova*.
1849	Arrested because of his participation in the "Petrashevsky Circle," a reading group interested in liberal and socialist ideas. Tried and sentenced to be shot. The sentence is commuted (on the field of execution) to four years of hard labor and four years in the army in Siberia.
1857	Marries Maria Dmitrievna Isaeva in Kuznetz, Siberia.
1858	Released from the service. *Uncle's Dream.*
1859	Permitted to return to St. Petersburg after ten years absence. *Selo Stepanchikovo.*
1861–62	*The Insulted and Injured* and *Notes from the House of the Dead.* Edits the journal *Time (Vremya).*
1862	First trip abroad.
1863	*Winter Notes on Summer Impressions. Time* shut down on official order. Second trip abroad.
1864	Death of his wife and his brother, M. M. Dostoevsky. Publication of *Notes from the Underground* in *Epoch (Epokha)*, a new journal edited by Dostoevsky.
1865	*Epoch* suppressed by government. *Crime and Punishment* and *The Gambler* (1866). Third trip abroad.
1867	Marries Anna Grigorievna Snitkina. Fourth trip abroad. Remains in Europe for four years.
1868	*The Idiot*
1870	*The Eternal Husband*
1871–72	Return to St. Petersburg. *The Devils.*
1873	Begins publication of *Diary of a Writer. A Gentle Creature.*
1874	First of a number of short trips in the 1870s to the health spa in Bad Ems, Germany.
1875	*The Raw Youth*
1876–77	Continuation of *Diary of a Writer* (interrupted in 1873).
1880	*The Brothers Karamazov*
1881	Death of Dostoevsky, January 28.

Notes on the Editor and Contributors

ROBERT LOUIS JACKSON (b. 1923), the editor of this volume, is professor of Russian Literature at Yale University. He is the author of *Dostoevsky's Notes from the Underground in Russian Literature* (1958) and *Dostoevsky's Quest for Form: A Study of His Philosophy of Art* (1966). He is also editor of *Chekhov: A Collection of Critical Essays* (1967).

KONSTANTIN MOCHULSKY (1892–48) was an emigré Russian scholar who lived in Paris. His books include *Gogol* (1934), *Dostoevsky* (1947), *Blok* (1948), *Bely* (1952).

VADIM V. KOZHINOV (b. 1930) is a Soviet Russian scholar. He is a senior research fellow at the Gorky Institute of World Literature in Moscow. He has written studies on the theory of literature, the origins of the novel, genre, and other subjects.

JACQUES MADAULE (b. 1895) is a French Catholic historian and literary critic. His numerous studies include *Le drame de Paul Claudel* (1936), *Dante et la splendeur italienne* (1957), *Le drame albigeois et le destin français* (1961), *Claudel et le langage* (1968).

NICHOLAS M. CHIRKOV (1891–50) was a Soviet Russian scholar. He was a lecturer in Russian and world literature at the N. K. Krupskaya Pedagogical Institute in Moscow. His study on Dostoevsky was published posthumously (1964, 1967).

NICHOLAS BERDYAEV (1874–48), the distinguished Russian philosopher and religious thinker, emigrated to Europe after the Bolshevik Revolution. His many books, translated into English and other languages, include *The Destiny of Man* (1937), *The Origins of Russian Communism* (1937), *Solitude and Society* (1938), *Dream and Reality* (1950).

ALFRED L. BEM [BOEHM] (1886– ?), a Russian scholar, came to Prague after the Bolshevik Revolution. Bibliographer and author of essays on Dostoevsky, Pushkin, and other writers, he disappeared after the liberation of Prague in 1945.

JOSEPH FRANK (b. 1918), American scholar and literary critic, is Professor of Comparative Literature at Princeton University. He is the author of *The Widening Gyre* (1963) and numerous essays on Dostoevsky and other writers.

F. I. EVNIN (b. 1909) is a Soviet Russian scholar. He has written extensive essays on Dostoevsky's novels.

YURY F. KARYAKIN (b. 1932) is a Soviet Russian scholar. He is a research fellow at the Institute of the International Labor Movement in Moscow, has written a book and several essays on Dostoevsky.

KONRAD ONASCH (b. 1916), a German, is professor of Theology at the Martin Luther University (Halle-Wittenberg) in Halle, German Democratic Republic. His various studies include *Das Weihnachtsfest in Orthodoxen Kirchenjahr* (1958), *Ikonen* (1961),

Grundzüge der Russischen Kirchengeschichte (1967), *Gross Nowgorod und das Reich der Heiligen Sophie* (1969).

ARON Z. STEINBERG (b. 1891), Russian emigré writer, is author of two studies on Dostoevsky.

JAMES M. HOLQUIST (b. 1935), an American, is associate professor of Russian Literature at Yale University. He has written essays on Russian and general literature.

Selected Bibliography on Crime and Punishment

Blackmur, R. P. "*Crime and Punishment*: Murder in Your Own Room." In *Eleven Essays in the European Novel*, pp. 119–140. New York: Harcourt Brace & World, Inc., 1964.

Fanger, Donald. "Apogee: *Crime and Punishment*." In *Dostoevsky and Romantic Realism*, pp. 184–213. Cambridge, Mass.: Harvard University Press, 1965.

Gibian, George. "Traditional Symbolism in *Crime and Punishment*." PMLA 70 (Dec., 1955): 979–96.

———, ed. *Feodor Dostoevsky: Crime and Punishment*. The Coulson Translation. Backgrounds and Sources. Essays in Criticism. New York: W. W. Norton Co., Inc., 1964.

Ivanov, Vyacheslav. "The Revolt Against Mother Earth." In *Freedom and the Tragic Life. A Study in Dostoevsky*. Translated by Norman Cameron [from the German] and edited by S. Konovalov, pp. 70–85. New York: The Noonday Press, 1952.

Meijer, J. M. "Situation Rhyme in a Novel of Dostoevskij." *Dutch Contributions to the Fourth International Congress of Slavicists*, 115–128. 'S-Gravenhage: Mouton & Co., 1958.

Mochulsky, Konstantin. "*Crime and Punishment*." In *Dostoevsky: His Life and Work*. Translated from the Russian by Michael A. Minihan, pp. 270–313. Princeton: Princeton University Press, 1967.

Mortimer, Ruth. "Dostoevski and the Dream." *Modern Philology* 54 (November, 1956), 106–116.

Rahv, Philip. "Dostoevsky in *Crime and Punishment*." *Partisan Review* 27 (Summer, 1960): 393–425.

Simmons, Ernest J. "In the Author's Laboratory," "Raskolnikov" and "The Art of *Crime and Punishment*." In *Dostoevsky: The Making of a Novelist*, pp. 139–183. London-New York: Oxford University Press, 1940.

Snodgrass, W. D. "*Crime and Punishment*: The Tenor of Part One." *Hudson Review* 13 (1960): 203–253.

Wasiolek, Edward. "*Crime and Punishment*." In *Dostoevsky: The Major Fiction*, pp. 60–84. Cambridge, Mass.: The M.I.T. Press, 1964.

———, ed. *Crime and Punishment and the Critics*. San Francisco: Wadsworth Pub. Co., 1961.

———, ed. *The Notebooks for Crime and Punishment*. Edited and translated, with an introduction, by Edward Wasiolek. Chicago & London: The University of Chicago Press, 1967.